POETOPIA

LONDON

Edited by Luke Chapman

First published in Great Britain in 2015 by:

Remus House
Coltsfoot Drive
Peterborough
PE2 9BF
Telephone: 01733 890066
Website: www.youngwriters.co.uk

Book Design by **ASHLEY JANSON**

SB ISBN 978-1-78443-869-2

Printed and bound in the UK by BookPrintingUK
Website: www.bookprintinguk.com

FOREWORD

Welcome, Reader!

For Young Writers' latest competition, Poetopia, we gave secondary school pupils nationwide the challenge of writing a poem based on the rules of one of 5 factions: Castitas for reflective, honest poetry; Temperantia for angry, assertive poetry; Humilitas for positive, uplifting poetry; Benevolentia for emotional poetry; and Industria for diligent, structured poetry. Poets who wrote a poem outside of these parameters were assigned to Dissimilis.

We chose poems for publication based on style, expression, imagination and technical skill. The result is this entertaining collection full of diverse and imaginative poetry, which is also a delightful keepsake to look back on in years to come.

Here at Young Writers our aim is to encourage creativity in the next generation and to inspire a love of the written word, so it's great to get such an amazing response, with some absolutely fantastic poems. Once all the books in the series are published we will pick the best poem from each faction to win a prize.

I'd like to congratulate all the young poets in **Poetopia - London** - I hope this inspires them to continue with their creative writing. And who knows, maybe we'll be seeing their names on the best seller lists in the future...

Jenni Bannister

Jenni Bannister
Editorial Manager

THE FACTIONS

CASTITAS (Kas-ti-tas)

- Write a soul-baring, honest poem
- Tell us what it is like to be you
- Channel your confusion and emotions at being a teenager into verse

TEMPERANTIA (Temper-ran-tee-ah)

- Stand up for someone or something
- Vent your anger through poetry
- Express your frustration about a situation that's out of your control

HUMILITAS (Hu-mil-lih-tahs)

- Write a positive, uplifting poem
- Write an ode to celebrate someone or something that you appreciate
- Write a spiritual poem

BENEVOLENTIA (Ben-e-vol-en-tee-ah)

- Write a love / emotional poem
- Empathise with another's situation or predicament
- Write a praise poem
- Write a poem about your best friend / your friendship

INDUSTRIA (In-dust-ree-ah)

- Write a poem about current affairs
- Use a strict poetic form, such as a sonnet or kyrielle
- Research a poet of your choice and write in a similar style

DISSIMǏLIS (Diss-i-mǐl-is)

- If pupils write a poem that falls outside of the factions' rules, they become Dissimǐlis
- Poems can be on any theme or style

CONTENTS

THE ELMGREEN SCHOOL, LONDON

WHITEFIELD SCHOOL, LONDON

THE POEMS

Money

M aximum madness
O n top of the world
N o one can stop me, I'm invincible
E lders they want me, children they love me
Y es, yes, yes that's the way for money!

Islam Saidani (12)
Central Foundation Boys' School, London

Ebola

Ebola has been going on for ages
If it was a book it would have a lot of pages.
The locals are dying
And the English aren't even trying.

They need to help those people out
But they're just messing about.
When the English get it
This is why they're having a fit.

When it comes back home
People start to change their tone.
But when it goes back there
People don't even care,
I think it's unfair.

The children have nowhere to go
And the government are staying low.
They need love
But they're going above.

Fabien Graham (12)
Central Foundation Boys' School, London

Sonnet To Nick Clegg

From the tangles of a powerless power,
You emerged confident, in this urgent fight,
But in the night, in a crippling hour,
Your party fell until the morning light.
You stood down, you did surrender,
Nobly thine power thou did forsake,
Not as noble to imagine, to render,
Fields of orange, blue as a lake,
But fair Nicholas please remember,
All is not lost, your great cause is fair,
Liberty swam in the heart of each member,
The guilt of tuition fees still linger there,
Alas this, but an election disaster,
Mr Nick Clegg is no longer our master.

Jon Griffin (12)
Central Foundation Boys' School, London

Untitled

Every day nowadays is so saturated, filled with the same stuff over and over again.
Is it that bad that I yearn for something different?
We're all content with 'okay', we don't have the fire to push ourselves to the limit as our ancestors did.
We're alright with mediocrity and it will never go away.
Unless we do something to ignite fire long gone . . .

Kwabena Adu-Ntiamoah (14)
Platanos College, London

To Hear This News

9 months in your belly
I don't think I'm ready
To hear this news.

Mother, Mum, Mummy
That was her name
I used to be ashamed
But she was the one to blame
I was 14 years old
To hear this news.

That my mother has cancer
18 months left
I don't get rest from all this stress
How could this be?
To hear this news.

Stress building up
I can't take this no more
How can she die?
And it's not a lie
To hear this news.

Dedicated to my mum.

An Ngo (14)
Platanos College, London

The Beautiful Voice

You swam in the sea of perpetual dreams
Of perpetual possibilities
So young and wide-eyed.

The turquoise waters enthralling
Lulling and lulling the waves went
Back and forth
You got lost in the thrill of achievement.

A beautiful voice called to you on the shore
Someone who never dared
To set foot in the sea of endless dreams
And possibilities.

You'll never make it, they say
Stop trying and just stay
How could you
So ordinary and simple
Do something so great?
Stay here with me
They said.

Cursed be the moment that you
Listened to them
Stopped before you even reached
The finish line
You forgot how to swim
Forgot how to dream
And also forgot that
If you don't swim
You drown.

And that beautiful voice on the shore
Watched you go down
With ugly triumph in their eyes.

And you couldn't save yourself
Because your eyes no longer
Imagined a colourful future
And your soul joined the
Innumerous others that
Wandered and never found.

Too scared to dream or to try
The once curious and wide-eyed child
Was bound by the bleak bars
Of your own prison.

Andressa Costa (14)
Platanos College, London

Joy

Joy is everywhere she goes
There's always a spring in her step
She smiles and laughs
And never plays hard
And when she's sad
Her soft expression
Gets turned upside down
But because she's filled
To the brim with joy
It's not that hard
To bring her back down
Into her home
With her friends and family
Right where she belongs
To put a smile on everyone's face
It's good we have her in our lives
To bring into our lives
That little thing that everyone needs
The little thing that is joy.

Jasmine Scott (12)
Platanos College, London

Insane

As I lay here,
On my bed.
I can hear voices,
That are in my head.
I can see things,
That no one else can see.
There is a face,
Smiling right at me.
In a blink of an eye,
It changes shape.
Now I'm in too deep,
There is no escape.
It looks like a devil,
I get so afraid.
I run to the toilet,
I feel so betrayed.
I lock the door,
And close my eyes.
I cannot stand,
All of these lies.
I open my eyes,
Everything gets worse.
It will not stop,
This must be a curse.
There she is,
Sitting right beside me.
I don't deserve this,
Just let me free.
Why did you pass away,
Without sending a letter.
I swear I helped but,
I could have treated you better.
Why do you haunt me?
I did my best
To help you survive,
You just needed to rest.
You didn't take my advice,
So it's not my fault.
Just leave me alone,

I'm not the one buried in a vault.
She's scaring my soul,
I'm so petrified.
In a matter of seconds,
I thought that I died.
I wake up in bed,
This was just a bad dream.
I feel so happy,
That I could scream.
I went to the toilet,
To find the mirror full of blood.
I must still be dreaming,
Until I hear a thud.
No! No! No!
This cannot be happening!
I'm not insane!
Why are you dismantling?
She comes in sight,
To scare me again.
Please tell me,
What you attain.
She lays there in bed,
With an evil smile on her face.
You're not as seducing,
So give me some space!
I cannot be afraid anymore,
This is now my daily life.
But who really cares,
If I have lost my wife?
I'm sorry my love,
But this has got to end.
Either you leave,
Or I'll descend.
She doesn't listen,
So there's only one way.
To make my life different,
Starting from today.
I get a wrinkly piece of paper,
And a very old pen.
I hold my breath,
And count to ten.
Right now,
I feel like I'm dead.

But it was always,
Inside my bloody head.
As I write my letter,
I thought for a bit.
To know what I could do,
Something bad I had to commit.
I caught hold of a rope,
And a stool.
I tied it around my neck,
I felt like a fool.
My wife reappeared,
Begged me to stay.
I don't love you anymore,
So please go away.
As I cried my last tears,
As I lived my last life.
I knew this was the end,
There's no need for a knife.
I stood on the stool,
Remembered my mates.
I thought of my child,
That had a terrible fate.
I caught the courage,
And so I let go.
I jumped off the stool,
And now I know.
That life,
Wasn't really meant to be.
Some people have to die,
And now I know I'm free.

Erica Dos Santos Seabra (14)
Platanos College, London

When We See A Bully

When I see a bully,
I make sure they never bully again,
I make sure that they will think again,
About what to do.

When I see a bully,
I tell them,
'What did they ever do to you?'
But they don't say anything back.

When I see a bully,
I make sure they run as if they are cheetahs,
I make sure they see what they are doing,
I make sure it is like I am the one controlling them.

When I see a bully,
I stand up for the victim,
I make sure the victim is not scared anymore,
I create a world where bullying is no longer a thing.

When you see a bully,
You should make sure they never bully again,
You should stand up for yourself,
To scare the bully away.

So when we see a bully,
We must become lions . . . tough and brave,
We must make sure no more bullies exist,
We must warn the teacher that bullying is taking place.

And once we do that . . .
Bullying will become a thing of the past.

Joel Philip Madeira Oliveira (13)
Platanos College, London

Why War?

Why war?
Did it have to start?
It took our family,
This broke our heart.
Why war?
Did they have to shoot all those guns?
Just so that they would have won.
Why war?
What is wrong with us?
Because of this we have lost all trust.
Why war?
Can we not see?
We should all get along,
Like family.
Why war?
We should not believe,
In fighting to get power which is terrible greed.
Why war?
Haven't we had enough?
Why can't we just learn to love?
War is horrible,
We should agree,
Then the world won't be as cruel as it can be.
Why war?
War is whack, just cut the world some slack.

Chloe Rowhan (12)
Platanos College, London

Sunshine

She's a little bit of sunshine to brighten my day,
Her warm smile is such a pleasure to display,
Who will fill our years with laughter,
And we'll live happily ever after.
Sunshine, sunshine in the air,
Sunshine you make the people stare.

Rabiah Mohammad (12)
Platanos College, London

Hajj (1937-2015)

Why did you have to die?
I never thought this day would come . . .
You made me feel special
You treated me like I was the only one . . .

I felt so free with you by my side
Like I could tell you anything
But now time has run out
And you are hearing the angels sing

I will always love you
And I cannot let you go
It is like my heart has been shot with a silver bullet
But I know one day we will say, 'Hello!'

Your time has come now
And I wish to see you again in Africa
But now it is too late
For me, just say, 'Hello!' to Auntie Aminah

I love you so much Grandad!

Aminah N'Gbale (12)
Platanos College, London

Taking A Stand

Taking a stand
Is to understand
To understand you should speak your mind
Against injustice and the unkind.

Humans are built to destroy
It's funny isn't it
How we think everything is our toy.

It's funny isn't it
How we can waste our food
While there's people with barely anything to eat.

It's funny isn't it
How we sleep safe and sound at night
When there's people afraid it's their last night.

It's funny isn't it
The girl you cuss in class to impress your friend
She cuts herself, it's legit
It will have no end,
She told me once.

But can you see emotions through the eyes
Because the feeling I got was of despair and loneliness.

Take a stand
And take the time
To donate to charities in command
Of stopping war, world hunger and bullying.

Take a stand
And give the girl a smile
A smile, a hug, a friendship . . .
Two weeks passed
And the girl no longer cutting herself
The bullies have been trashed
And you have a true friendship.

A smile will go a mile
Who will take a stand if not you?
Him, her and you
All together could put a stop
And exercise equality
To all humanity.

Marta Mateus (14)
Platanos College, London

We're All Different

We're all different,
Kids get distressed and scared,
Simply because they're stared.
Words that they say hurt,
More than if you were burnt.
Thinking scars could take away the pain,
But you're just going insane.
Silence takes over you,
Faking a smile,
Just to make it one more mile.
But she can make it through it,
She just has to wait a bit.
She didn't let them bring her down,
And no one else made a sound.
When . . .
She wrote a song,
That helped others stay strong.
And that was the end.
Just remember,
No matter how bad
Or hard the situation is,
You can rise above it.
And you can win it.

Lara Lagoas-Dos Santos (14)
Platanos College, London

Life

Life is a gift
That can put you in a bit of a twist
Anything that you do will stay
In your mind till that unfortunate day
Memories come but never go
Although they may be bad
You should live life like you've never had a bad day.

Life opens up new doors
That can sometimes find you being on the floor
No matter what you do
There will always be someone that loves you
At different stages of life
You will get different advice
No matter what others say
Always go the way you say in your prayers.

Life is like a plant
It grows and becomes more advanced
Once it has reached its peak
It will blossom real neat
You can never learn enough
So try and gain some trust.

Life is a gift
So you try your best not to lose it
No matter what happens
There will always be some sort of pattern.

Life is a gift so why don't you use it
Why don't you take a glance
So you can see more in advance.

Yesterday was history
Tomorrow is a mystery
But now is a gift
That's why it is called present.

Life is a gift
And you should remember it.

Payam Mohammed (14)
Platanos College, London

Love

It's strange,
The slightest touch may make you feel woozy,
It glistens in the sunlight like a freshly cut diamond,
It can be seen at first sight no matter the range.

It may be broken,
By the jealousy of others,
As soon as you lost the love of your life, you were awoken,
'I lost my love for you,' she mutters.

As the pain is indescribable,
You have left me here praying with a Bible,
Before we always used to play,
Now me crying in my bed is where I lay.

Rodrigo Branco (14)
Platanos College, London

Valentine

Roses are red, violets are blue,
This is how much I feel for you,
Our hearts are together as one,
I cannot be away from you for too long.

I took your heart, you took mine,
As I look at you, your eyes shine.
You are now part of my soul,
You make me a whole.

Believe me, I love you with all my heart,
We shall never be put apart.

Tatiana Teofilo (12)
Platanos College, London

Monster

Trapped between four walls,
Soiled with red, some of mine and some before me.
I cry in terror, eyes glinting in the dark,
Of the fearsome being I have become.

My hands tremble, my body is unstable.
What exactly am I?
Am I human?
Or am I a monster?

Hands covered in dark crimson, eyes glistening gold.
Body covered in scars, suffering from 'conditioning'.
Eyes that have given up hope – living with no purpose.
Ears like a cat, tail like a cat, claws like a cat.

What am I?
I am human.
No one believes me.
Cat-like features make me inhuman – a monster in their eyes.

Katherine Chan (12)
Platanos College, London

I Give

I give you this present,
To replicate our love,
You are my gift,
My gift from God,
So in return,
I present to you,
The gift of my love,
Forever to be true.

Sharae Roxanne Nevers (12)
Platanos College, London

I Don't Know

I don't know what to write
I've found myself in a plight
But know now I've seen the light
I know what to scribble down
And I'll buy and wear a winning gown
Then charge victoriously through the night.

I don't know what to think
About this terrible event
I wish I could shout and repent
And say whatever comes into my head
But then I'll know I've let myself down
Then be taken of my golden crown.

I don't know what to play
I've been thinking about it all day
There is nothing else than to sit down
And entertain myself in a special way.

Now there are a lot of things you and I don't know
And everyone knows this is very true
In outer space or in the human race
So goodbye my friends
And enjoy your weekend
So hope that time comes to its very end.

Wait, don't leave yet
I don't know why I'm still writing this
I'm so sorry that this won't rhyme
But I'm running out of time . . .

Tyrese Obika (12)
Platanos College, London

The Flight Of Life

Thirty eggs, in the tree marking the start of Life Road, hatched.
Thirty birds, ready to start, jumped from their nests.
Their parents glided alongside them,
But at eighteen metres, they fell back.

The thirty birds flew on, gracefully.
The waiting hunters below raised their guns, automatically.
Everyone had a name.
Ignorance, Stubbornness and Aggression, just to name a few.
Their guns fired.
About ten of the birds fell from the sky.
The remaining flew on, aware of what had happened.

The flock had now reached about twenty-five metres.
The birds were hungry.
They landed in a large clearing,
Filled with many new, exotic fruits and plants.
Some looked the same but were completely different.
Most ate and restored their strength.
Some wandered into a dark, mysterious hole which led to the jaws of a fox called Temptation.
While eating, the birds encountered another flock.
The two groups mingled until it was time to leave.
The flocks exchanged members.
Then the two flocks went their separate ways.

Once in the air again, the flock continued to fly down the road.
But near halfway, the next wave of hunters struck.
These ones had names like Loss, Depression, Anger or Guilt.
Again, most of the flock fell to the ground, unmoving.
Yet there were more hunters still.
The ground was littered with lifeless birds.
The survivors could see the end of the road:
A cliff overlooking a bright blue sea, leading to a golden sky.
Only two birds remained.
They flew alongside each other, looking towards their goal.
One last hunter called Misfortune, raised his gun.
The shot rang loud and clear.

White feathers, stained with blood, drifting on the wind.
The last bird out of thirty, cleared Life Road.
Flying high out over the cliff, she rose into the golden sky.

Leo Schrey-Yeats
St Aloysius' College, London

Humans

It is so easy to die,
But so hard to live.
It is so easy to cry,
But so hard to forgive.
It is so easy to hate,
But so hard to love.
It's so easy to retaliate,
But hard to rise above.
It's so easy to lose,
But so hard to win.
It's so easy to win,
But so hard to lose.
It's so easy to sin,
But so hard to use,
To use our minds,
Instead we use our bodies,
We use them for aggression.
We do not use our words,
Instead we create depression.
We are humans, we make mistakes,
But we can forget them simply by eating cakes.
We are humans, we create,
But in the end we make mistakes.

Jesse Mukose (13)
St Aloysius' College, London

Nicholas' Poem

I look around,
And I see nothing,
I look around,
And I start to cry,
I look around,
And I ask myself why?
Why do I look around to see my life?
My life is everywhere,
I'm just yet to see it,
But when it comes,
I know I'll see it,
All I need,
Is to just be patient,
And when my life comes,
I'll look around.

Nicholas Keane
St Aloysius' College, London

Dear David Cameron

We are the age of the broken, the wounded, the dying.
We are the age of tumours, corruption and lying.
We are the age of the wrong, the foul and the perverse.
We are the age that pairs religion with hate and science with adoration.
We are the age of fear, war and despair.
We are the age of debt, worry and fraud.
You were the age meant to save us.
You were the age that failed us.

Mason Clancy
St Aloysius' College, London

The Walls Are Closing In

The walls are closing in.
The walls are laughing, mocking me.
An iron fist knocks at my door,
Paralysed.
The walls are insulting me.
The words piercing my heart.
Bleeding inside.
The iron fist is breaking my door.
I still can't move.
The walls are striking me,
Knocking me around.
The iron fist is through the door,
Heading straight for me.
Helpless to defend myself,
I submit to its iron will.

David Udoh (14)
St Aloysius' College, London

Red

Molten hatred was my blood, travelling through my veins.
Deep inside that inflicts pain, agony, despair.
The heat caused my blood to boil.
Words that cannot be spoken.
A love that is trapped, fuelled by embers of hate.
A flame burns in my soul and scorches my heart.
Agony that lights me aflame.
Red.

Bartek Gwara (14)
St Aloysius' College, London

What I Can See

I see a hill,
But think of a mountain.
I see a spring,
But think of a fountain.

I see a lake,
But think of the sea.
I see a sapling,
But think of a tree.

I see some mist,
But think of a cloud.
I see a group,
But think of a crowd.

I see a sheep,
But think of a flock.
I see a port,
But think of a dock.

I see myself,
But look beyond me.
I've found myself,
What I can be.

Dominic Kitson (14)
St Aloysius' College, London

Hidden

The city may look so vibrant and lovely,
But everything here isn't as it may seem,
Every corner you turn,
Hostility, hurt, hate and burn.

'Unpaid worker, immigrant, terrorist'
Even some 'friends' beginning to assist,
But still at home, no peace of mind see,
I try so hard to put all of it behind me.

At home no emotion can flow,
Have to be strong, so I let it go,
Put on a smile, make her happy,
Better that than let her worry.

No one to give me comfort, no one to talk to,
Pray, wish, hope, that's all I really can do,
Ask the one above watching over me,
With him I find a timely sanctuary.

I reflect and remember the words she told me,
So long ago, a time where I had some safety,
'Go to school, don't fight, work your hardest,
Grow up to be good, Godly and honest.'

That's why I will never fight back,
Never return a punch or an attack,
I may look dark, distressed or defeated,
But know that inside I am completed.

Sakib Hussain (13)
St Aloysius' College, London

My Progression Of Life

Since I was young,
I've been out in the sun,
I've been through lots of fun,
And my life so far I have loved,
The beat of a drum,
Motivates me like a bullet in a gun,
To progress with the triumph,
That I've tried, failed and done.

So far, I've done well,
And that makes my life swell,
I guess I can tell,
Pains that hurt like hell,
All the times I fell,
But I have accomplished enough to yell,
I have used all senses: sight, hearing, tasting, touching and smell,
And I have seen dreams come or melt.

The progression of life,
Makes me try and try,
To accomplish tasks I would like,
And try new things in near sight,
I will have to fight,
To get near to the lies,
So I can grab the glow of the light,
And get to those all-time highs.

Hector Cayo Jorro (13)
St Aloysius' College, London

Life

Everyday life,
Everyday challenges,
Trying to figure out,
What life's all about,
I'm lost in a world,
That I don't belong in,
My opinion doesn't matter,
My thoughts don't count,
Why can't I be noticed
While I'm walking around?

No one cares what I think,
No one cares what I'm talking about,
The only thing they come for,
Is themselves and shut me out,
I wanna be released,
From the jail I'm in now,
Where I'm not always hated,
But cherished all day round.

All those bullies when I was younger,
I overcame them as I went about,
Feeling alone,
In that dark gloomy corner,
I'm talking about my past,
As it's happening right now,
Overcoming those memories,
Overcoming those fears,
It's not so easy,
But as being myself,
I was never in doubt.

Abbas El-Zein (13)
St Aloysius' College, London

Strolling Down The Street

Skipping down the road in fresh, new shoes,
Passing the shop and I hear a cow moo,
Then when I am walking, I step in dog poo,
Now my day is ruined with lots of doo doo.

I change my shoes and put on boots,
And then I see a group of men wearing suits,
I pass a chicken shop and have to go in,
And when I'm full, I throw the box in the bin.

I walk out of the shop whistling a tune,
Then I look up at the sky and see the moon,
I wonder to myself if it is late,
Then I see £20 on the floor, it must have been fate.

Now I am strolling home,
And I see a cat in a big dome,
When I reach my door,
I wonder what more adventures lie for me.

Cameron Ocran (13)
St Aloysius' College, London

Her

Your lips so soft and red,
The thought of kissing you stuck in my head.
Your beauty so bright and warm,
Shining through the darkest storm.
A hidden feeling that grows stronger,
The time we're apart feels even longer.
As the days go,
I know where my heart glows.

Christopher Bolanos Betancur
St Aloysius' College, London

World At War

World at war
The war was horrendous
The guns were firing
Everyone was scared.

The Germans invaded
The British retaliated
The Russians barraged
The Americans were bombing.

The last stand
Germany are crushed to the ground
Russians invade Berlin
The war comes to an end.

In the Pacific, 1945
America has had it
They bomb Japan
Until they fall.

Jack Taylor (13)
St Aloysius' College, London

I Hate Writing Poetry

I absolutely hate it
Writing poetry
Anything I write never feels right
I can never wrap my head around it
Mostly because I am not good at it
It confuses me every time
And it's always hard to write the next line
Writing poetry takes too much of my time
Especially when I try to make it rhyme
I absolutely hate it
Writing poetry.

Casey Punter (13)
St Aloysius' College, London

Started From The Bottom Now He's Here

Holes the size of craters in the soles of his shoes!
He promised himself that he would improve.
This life of poverty is not for him!
Every night he would pray to the Lord for him to escape.
But he knew he had to have some faith!

As soon as he was twelve years old,
He would no longer be told!
Years of beating by the teachers!
They had taken their toll.
With bruises that were raw and sore.
He decided he could take no more!

He had heard that London was a great place.
Where the Irish men could show their face!
That was the place for him to go.
Start a new life and stay low.

The roaring sixties had arrived!
London continued to thrive,
He loved the people that he met,
People of colour and all they represent,
He learnt about other ways of life,
Listened to reggae and started to jive.

He worked all day and through the night,
Then he met his lovely wife!
She worked just as hard as him,
Together they shared the same dream,
To return home and live the dream.

Forty years later, they now live the dream,
They have homes and money beyond their dreams,
An inspiration they are to me,
I love them more than they can see.

Nanny and Grandad I love you so and cannot thank you any more!
You have known hardship more than most,
But you have never forgotten your roots.
Today I thank you for it all,
I love you, that is all.

Brandon Curran (12)
St Aloysius' College, London

A Certain Teacher

I travel to school every day
To learn something new and to play
All teachers are different, every single one
Either being funny, serious or simply dumb
But there's this certain teacher
Who comes number one.

We travel back in time from present to past
And do this whilst having a blast
Feeding us homework, slaving in class
Sometimes it's a right pain in the . . .
But this certain teacher takes it calmly
Even though our visit is timely.

This certain teacher has become much more
This teacher's a friend, that's what they're for
We discuss our ups and downs which can be sloppy
However, we do this over a coffee
Honestly, this teacher's like no other
And hate it when we have a cover.

This certain teacher's room is something to admire
Helping our levels get higher and higher
We do adore this teacher, oh so much
When teaching there's a special touch
In a way, this certain teacher guided me through
And to that I say thank you.

Oliver Langton (13)
St Aloysius' College, London

Forever Watching

Seldom remember
The dreams they have had
But do you want to remember?
Would you be so glad?

You think most of the time
You're happily dreaming
But do you remember
Why you were born screaming?

Oh, yes I was there
In your dreams, in your head
I shall watch you forever
I shall watch when you're dead.

Daniel Atherton (13)
St Aloysius' College, London

The Worst Love

A tear of joy,
A tear of sorrow,
They're both shed with love.

It starts crystal clear,
There in plain sight,
But darkness fills it quickly.

The love is left,
Abandoned and gone,
But death stays right here.

As there's nothing worse,
Than a lover's death,
And suicide is looming.

Tyler Flynn Maximen-Thornton (13)
St Aloysius' College, London

Dreams

Nothing is impossible,
Everything is possible,
Some people will doubt you,
Think you are a fool,
But you have to carry on,
The journey will be long,
You will get things wrong,
But it is all worth it,
If you do not quit,
Nothing is ever easy,
Everyone has to struggle,
Down the long tunnel,
There is always an obstacle in the way,
But that is not an excuse for you to say,
It is never too late for change in your life,
All you have to do is strive and strive,
And not waste time,
To accomplish your big dream!

Kevin Martinez (13)
St Aloysius' College, London

The Pool

Gazing at the glistening pool which dazzles in the moonlight,
Watching the fishes bring a bit of sparkle to the water,
Making it turn bright,
Should I look far and wide as to where to dive in,
Or,
Sit back and be amazed at this unique sight,
Because,
Now I know this brings a bit of happiness to my boring old life!

James Matthews (13)
St Aloysius' College, London

War, A Thing Of The Past

War, a thing of the past,
Many would have thought,
We didn't have any wars,
However, there are more than ever.

Many types of war,
Civil wars,
Legal wars,
But who would have thought,
We still had wars.

First World War,
Second World War,
Everyone thought,
We wouldn't have any more,
But now,
There are more,
Than ever before.

Why is it though?
Is it an addiction to war?
Is it jealousy or do they want power?
It's neither of those,
Why? Because it's always
A different type of war.

Ignacio Laval (13)
St Aloysius' College, London

Fading Nature

Nature, so full of wonder, so full of grace
Life flourishes
Within its embrace

Nature, and its motherly face
Set a graceful welcome
For the human race

Nature, filled with inspirations
Trees, plants and animals
Majestic creations

But humans, no respect or care
Strip the lands and forests bare
With machines and fast-growing flares

Nukes and wars tear countries apart
Rids nature of its beauty
Shattering its heart

Nature, now miserable, hopeless and dim
Foul liquid oozes
from where fishes used to swim

Animals suffer in despair
Hopeless and homeless
Cos humans don't care

Those scars will not mend
Chaos will descend
When the time comes, that'll be the end

Jacky Lee
St Aloysius' College, London

World War One

When Germany invaded,
On the night of the war,
Russians attacked,
The Germans no more.

Deep in a trench,
It's full of mice,
The army of French,
Covered in lice.

On came the British,
Determined to win,
The Germans get finished,
After this sin.

Finally, the French,
Meet up with the British,
They sit in a trench,
This poem is finished.

Emre Ustun (12)
St Aloysius' College, London

Fear

A darkness takes over,
It spreads the anxiety,
The nightmare engulfs you,
Lost and alone,
Running from home,
A freakish mill,
On a silent hill,
Your unheard shout,
But no one's about,
Something wants you dead,
And you are off your head,
You want to be home with an apple pie,
But you're in a corner waiting to die.

Jasi Seyahoei (13)
St Aloysius' College, London

I Hate

I hate hypocrites
But not as much as politics
Conservatives, you must be having a laugh
David Cameron is a wannabe
Politicians are funny
No, they're just dummies.

I hate popularity
But not as much as humiliation
I like books
But hate crooks
It's not every day crybabies fighting
How about just have a night in.

I hate talks
But not as much as deep thoughts
I hate my brothers and sisters
But not as much as my broken scissors
Cold nights
Foggy days.

I hate them all.

Joshua Okot (13)
St Aloysius' College, London

My Life

Getting bullied is contagious
With my heart full of the opposite of gracious.

Getting called dumb and wrong
Just makes me want to sing a hateful song.

Listening to music keeps me calm and steady
But the hate is keeping me heavy.

The warm hug from my parents
Make me think my bullies are peasants.

Having friends side to side
Forcing enemies to hide.

Teachers telling me info
Persuade me to use it as my YouTube intro.

As we near the end of this work
I just want to say that I really don't like homework.

Dan Gatchalian (13)
St Aloysius' College, London

Untitled

We kept a secret,
You couldn't keep it.
You told the whole school
What had happened, now we are through.
You were my friend,
My only friend.
The one I could trust,
But I guess not.
You turned against me and left me alone down in the dark,
We promised it would be forever, said we'd never part.
Now you chose to walk away, away in the dark,
I hope one day I can just close my eyes and fade away.

Kylie Ferrer (11)
St James' Catholic High School, London

I Thought We Were Close

We went to a different school
We met in class
I tried to get to know you
But you pushed me away
I see you with your friends
I see you with my friends
But not with me
I know you like her
I know she likes you
You know all about her
But nothing about me
I like you
But do you like me?

Taina Ramnuth (11)
St James' Catholic High School, London

God Our Father

Sending prayers to God our Father
Someone that loves one another
Someone that would give forgiveness
Someone that would share kindness

Sending prayers to God our Father
Someone that looks over others
Someone that we would worship
Someone that would share his friendship.

Samson Wilson Rojas Liu (12)
St James' Catholic High School, London

Temperantia

What would you do if I told you
About the years I have struggled and survived through?
What would you do if I said
About the days I could never go to bed?
How about the days I have had stress
Nearly leading to my death?
If you share this,
Don't despair,
Because you are stronger than this,
You can survive it.
Whenever you feel alone, with nowhere to go,
Spend time with family or friends at home.
But remember,
Friends come and go,
Family doesn't,
So don't walk away, like your life has blown away,
Listen to your instinct,
So you don't regret anything.

Sophie Kagan (13)
St Marylebone CE School, London

My Story

If only people could see,
The truth that lies within me,
The story behind my depression and pain,
The force and pressure of having weight gain,
Being monitored and watched as if a baby,
And always having to hear the words 'eventually' or 'maybe'.

If only people really knew,
What too much of anything could do to you,
Perhaps that's how I got so far,
Not realising that my body needs food just like petrol for a car,
They cannot move on an empty tank,
And with the use of this knowledge, I have many people to thank.

Sometimes my brain feels as if it could pop,
As all of my physical activity I have had to stop,
No dance, no running, no commitment or fun,
Yet no one else can be blamed for what I've done,
You would think I'd enjoy not having to do anything and rest,
But to be honest, I hate it as much as I hate a test.

It's scary to think how close I was to death,
Who would have thought that exercise could affect your breath?
I tried to pretend to my friends that everything was OK,
And, of course, they did not have much they could say,
But the truth is that I am scared of what I have become,
I just wish that this wicked time could be redone.

It is going to affect me for the rest of my life,
All because of my brain becoming so rife,
I did to myself such terrible damage,
Yet it did not stop me and I was still able to manage,
Which is why I found it so hard to understand,
That suffering and pain is a part of this land.

Having sacrificed months of hard work and time,
I have to rebuild my strength and learn how to climb,
But now I am ready for my story to be told,
So that people will never have to experience what it's like to be so cold,
You cannot understand how hard it was to write this,
So pease do not let this message be one you miss.

Sidney Tucker (14)
St Marylebone CE School, London

Titanium

Uriah straps me in,
There is no turning back,
I hover, high, at the top of the skyscrapers,
Someone asks me, 'Do you feel sturdy?'
I feel strong, like titanium . . .

They push me, I am flying,
I can't even feel my harness,
I am free as the wind gushes through my hair,
I shut my eyes and scream with joy,
I feel strong, like titanium . . .

Invincible, no one could touch me,
Unstoppable, I have no limit,
Dauntless, I finally belong,
Speechless, I was in my element,
I feel strong, like titanium . . .

I throw my hands to the side,
I am confident in myself for the first time,
Exhilarated, this is a memory I will never forget,
I forget everything that has happened,
I feel strong, like titanium.

Neena Sara Taj (12)
St Marylebone CE School, London

Temperantia

I was angry and I shall not pretend,
I told my wrath, my wrath did end.
I was angry at it though,
I told it not, my wrath did grow.

And it showed both day and night,
Till it gave my friends a fright.
And my enemy beheld its shine,
And he knew that it was mine.

And into my garden it goes,
I have to hide it, it cannot show.
In the morning, glad, I see,
Anger is just beneath the tree.

Siang Tan (12)
St Marylebone CE School, London

Happiness

Happiness is like a butterfly.
Happiness is a direction.
Happiness is living in the present moments.
Everyone said stay happy because happiness is life and if you live without happiness,
Your life will not be very easy.
As living without happiness is not living at all.
If you have had a life without happiness,
Try make your happiness by doing things that make you happy.

Rawdah (12)
Southfields Academy, London

Poetry!

Not everyone gets it right the first time
Success is unfortunately a wicked and difficult climb
For those who just won't lose hope
Success will throw down a life saving rope
Work hard, work smart and you will succeed
Don't follow the rest of the world, take the lead
We must carry on and be successful
Take pride in your work, no matter what
We must succeed
Success isn't just about what you accomplish in your life
It's about what you inspire others to do
Don't put a limit on anything
The more you dream, the further you get
Learning gives creativity
Creativity leads to thinking
Thinking provides knowledge
Knowledge makes you great
Education is the key to unlock the golden door of freedom
Education is a journey not a race
Teachers open the door but you must enter by yourself.

Shaqib Hussain (12)
Southfields Academy, London

Football

Will the ball be attached to my feet?
I dodged my enemy as I dribbled the ball through his legs like a sneaky snake dodges its enemy.
I was as fast as a bullet. I ran, I dribbled but am I going to score?
I . . . scored! I screamed like I was the leader of the pack of howling wolves.
Everyone was cheering to every player in my team
Especially me because I became man of the match!

Abdullah Abdullah (12)
Southfields Academy, London

My Summer Holidays

It was during my summer holidays
While my dad was working for a few days
My mum and I had some enjoyable days.

One early morning, I was at the seaside
With my mum on my side
Watching the sun rise.

Far on the horizon I could see
A boat passing in the high sea.

On the trees the birds were singing
I plunged into the sea and started swimming
My mum on the beach kept watching.

The water was a bit chill
I was worried that I might fall ill.

I was spending my time happily
While my mum was watching passionately.

This was a memorable moment of my life
That one day I will tell my wife.

Aneesh Sujore (12)
Southfields Academy, London

To Be Real

Aren't we supposed to treat our neighbours with love and respect?
But instead we discriminate and choose not to accept
And face the facts
And stop trying to act
That we aren't trapped and controlled
In a society that forces us to play specific roles
A negra
A killer
A born sinner
A non-believer
A drug dealer
I can always forgive but I've sworn to myself I can never forget!
I bet you remember the looting and vandalism
But I know you have blocked out the triggers and forgotten
How the police have brutally killed several peaceful men
Now and again
No inquiries, no justice
Loss of life and communities left feeling like hostages
Barricaded behind their own skin
With no hope, no win.
To be real . . . this is the unfortunate world we live in.

Abraham Olayiwola (16)
Southfields Academy, London

Me

You would not like to be me.
I am a tailspin of daggers.
Out of control, being thrown through hearts.

Trust me . . .
You would not like to be me!

Cuts on my arms.
Tears overflowing every night.
Hearing voices, seeing mocking stares.
Tormenting my soul every day.
I tried ending it all but I can't be that selfish.
I've already done enough.
Shame, humiliation and regret feeding through my body and spirit.

Dominating my brain and leaving me sleepless at nights.
I can't complain.
I deserve it.
This is me!

Alberta Oko-Agyemang (16)
Southfields Academy, London

My Jolly Poem

I always have jolly days at good old Southfields Academy.
I always like making new friends.
Funny friends, helpful friends,
And yes, weird ones too!
But for some reason I don't mind.
All I want is true friends that are trustworthy, kind and loyal.
And that's what true friends are.
That's what makes every day good.
And that is my happy and jolly life!

Mohamed Shafraz (11)
Southfields Academy, London

My Poem

When I go riding on my bike
There's lots of things that I like
The sky so blue
It makes me think
That summer is here
A time for everyone
To enjoy the fun
Of summertime
The best
Time of year.

Daniel Bale (12)
Southfields Academy, London

Happy

Unlock your dream
You only live life once
God
Thanks for everything beautiful
Please forgive me if I didn't
Like it
Sorry
Every bright day brings
A new opportunity to do
Better and better
Be ready because
You only live once.

Tahira Ahmad (12)
Southfields Academy, London

I Don't Know

Running, running away from this,
Clutching life with my little pinkie,
Wishing if only, if only this,
Would go away but I'm determined,
I'm strong,
Am I?
Yes, I am,
No, I'm not,
Yes, I am and I'll keep running, running away from this,
Grabbing hold of life with my two hands,
But still wishing, wondering when it will go,
I don't know.

Tiziri Hadjmahfoud (12)
Sydenham School, London

This Is Me

Silence.
Not a ruffle of a coat,
Or a cough from a child,
This was my moment.

I walked towards the light,
And the faces,
And the pleasure,
This is me.

The colourful butterflies,
Floating and dancing,
Words engraved into my brain,
Flooded out to the world.

This is me,
Drama,
This is me.

Jasmine Bourane (11)
Sydenham School, London

Mother's Love And Care

I believe in love at first sight,
Because I've been loving my mother since I've opened my eyes, that's right.
My love for her is further than the time it took,
For Armstrong to go to the moon and back.
Heavier than every loving soul, caring soul, human soul, weighed in a sack,
But it is tested by the venomous obstacles of life,
And by all the diverse dreams and goals that we strive for.

As we walk through our narrow
And twisting path of nature's way,
We forget the one that helped us reach
And stay on this path till this very day.
We know but yet we turn a blind eye,
I guess that's nature's way of leaving us all astray.

However, when our path comes to a bitter end,
We go running back to the one whose love has no bitterness nor bend.
Her welcoming smile makes our hearts
Shine with delicate lights.
Her company is what gets us to sleep at painful nights,
She hears my cries and wipes away my tears,
Tells me to love who I am, reassures all my fears.

A mother's love and care is
Something that no one can explain.
It is made of deep devotion and of sacrifice and pain.
It is endless and unselfish
And enduring come what may.
For nothing can destroy it or take that love away.

So people don't take for granted what you earn,
Through your mother's love and care,
For you will only know her true value, when you see her empty chair.

Amal Abubakar (12)
Sydenham School, London

Mum

Roses are red
The sky is blue
Mix it together
It makes you
Don't run away
Stay right here
The day of a death
Is the day of my birth
Running away
Is hell on Mars
I might want to kill you
But I really do love you
Your love is more than mine
I will never forget the day you die
For Mum
You are the light in stars
The worth in the sun
You're really young
Just 39
We all love you Mum.

Plamedie Tampo (12)
Sydenham School, London

Swim

Swim, swim, never stop.
Standing up on the diving block,
Striving to be the best.

Take your marks,
Go!
I dive,
I hear the crowds cheering,
Come on,
You can do it.

My arms and legs are flailing,
I'm going as fast as I can,
I'm speeding like a bullet,
Then I hit the wall.

It's over,
I've won!
All the training has paid off,
The crowds are shouting my name,
I'm smiling because I've done it,
Swim, swim, never stop.

Eliza Boddy (12)
Sydenham School, London

The Last Kiss

The pain you felt that day was the pain I felt when you were gone.
Every moment I was with you by that bed,
I was happy even though I knew you would go.
A tear flows through my eyes,
But I knew you wouldn't want me to be sad, you are fine.
Now I will remember every moment I had with you,
When you bathed me I would cry,
I never knew you would go,
I would have one last kiss goodbye.

Roanna Mitchell (12)
Sydenham School, London

The Ice Cream

Oh ice cream, oh ice cream,
How I do love you, ice cream,
You are as precious to me as any other food,
A smooth layer of crystallised goodness,
A soft layer of silk,
Different flavours bursting inside my mouth,
When I think about you, I always beam with joy,
Oh ice cream, oh ice cream,
How I do love you, ice cream.

Grace Ruth Quashie (12)
Sydenham School, London

What I Did For Love!

First we were strangers
Next we were mates
Why did you have to move houses
Was it because of the trust and doubt
You promised me one thing
That I would always be your love, life and heart
Why didn't you come back?
I made a search party but seems like it's nothing
I panicked with love to find you didn't come
But now I lay where I must stay today
This is what I did for our love.

Kadisha Gody (11)
Sydenham School, London

Fireworks

Bang! There goes another one,
Screaming as it goes
It's getting high
Up in the sky
And fizzle, there it blows
Whoosh! Up high above the house
Behind a trail of sparks
Yellow, orange
Red and white
Exploding in the dark.

Michaela Blane-Mitchell (12)
Sydenham School, London

Darkness

No light just dark
Not a single speck of light
Drip, drop is all you can hear
Drip, drop, drip, drop
From above the tunnel
I am trapped
Nowhere to go
No food to eat.

Only dirty puddles of water
Is all I drink
Too weak to talk
Even walk
I try to find an exit
But nowhere to be found.

All my friends are dead
No one left
I am the only one left
The only one who survived
Tears trickle down my face
I must stand alone and I must stay strong.

I stand up
But I just tremble down
Reaching for the sky
But I am still on the ground
I might not ever escape
And this may be my last sound
I lay in peace
My dignity still alive
I close my eyes
And count to 3
Because this may be
The last breath I breathe.

Samira Zara Ahmed (11)
Sydenham School, London

Fun Is Timeless

Fun is timeless,
Fun never fades away,
So swap the grey inside you,
For fun can be anything you say.

It could be watching TV,
Or living life on the edge,
But remember to share,
Because fun is rare
And you might not have it again.

Shaima Haider (12)
Sydenham School, London

About Us...

I am brave, confident and strong,
I am clever enough to tell right from wrong.
My clothes are dark,
I am afraid of sharks.
But I can tell right from wrong

Clever, courageous and cunning,
We are quite fast at running.
We are Dissimilis,
The best and most brilliant.
And that's who we are.

Kiyomi Sharna McKenzie (12)
Sydenham School, London

The Truth Of A Silhouette

It was the truth I thought,
My thoughts were caught.
First it was anxiety then curiosity,
But my mind remained tangled in philosophy.
I skipped, leapt and jumped down,
What was I expecting?
Four is who I found...
Actions disguised as consequences,
Consequences remained those tall, solid fences.
I stand tall, peering at my obstacles,
Yet I knew they bared lots of cause.
My growth was increasing,
Others were vigorously decreasing.
My own 'friend' turned against me,
As I was the undiscovered key-
Who could set humanity free.
I am divergent and yes, it is within me,
She herself just couldn't let me be free.

Gabby Mullings (14)
Sydenham School, London

The Life Of Love

I wipe a tear from my eye,
Wishing you were here.
I feel this pain on my left,
Like if someone was stabbing me.
I think about the dangers you're facing,
The gunshots you're hearing,
And the blood you're smelling,
Curse the war you're after.

Sara Gjokaj (14)
Sydenham School, London

The Innocent Heart

I have a pure heart
So much so I care too much
Darkness surrounds my sorrow heart
Like a dagger through my heart
My heart looked like a storm was brewing
As the beat of my heart slowly decreased
To a departure of long disbelief
As the beacon of hope gradually faded
Terror rushed like a stream of a thousand voices
As the pain comes to an end
And as the end draws near
The innocent heart goes to sleep.

Rebecca Ranjit (14)
Sydenham School, London

Curse The Man

She sat there for countless days,
Wondering, wondering if her love would ever come,
But like a dehydrated flower, she began to wilt,
I wanted to motivate her, to give her a reason to be persistent,
But I became doubtful, will he ever come?
My heart grew disgusted and angry,
No female should be left to feel this way,
Curse the man that left her to feel this way,
That left her to actually think love may come her way,
That left her to feel depressed and lonely,
That left her to blame herself for being naive,
That left her to feel worthless and irrelevant,
Curse the man that left her.

Wura Agoro (14)
Sydenham School, London

Happy Place

The relaxing sound
The waves crashing against the shore
The sun setting
Being slowly swallowed up by the sea
As the sky gets slightly darker
The air beginning to get colder
And the tide retreating
The place where it felt like the world had stopped for a second
It was as if the world was at peace
When I came here
And it gave me a feeling I have never felt before
I felt free and like I could do anything I wanted
It was my happy place.

Marina Pisano (14)
Sydenham School, London

Alone

Alone,
She was alone,
By herself, but not at home,
Crouched down by herself on the floor,
Nothing around her except the door,
Quietness was the only thing that accompanied her,
But she didn't want it to be with her,
How did she get here?
What did she do?
She didn't want to be here,
By herself,
Alone.

Keshalini Katpakanantha (13)
Sydenham School, London

Benevolentia

Wiping tears from my eyes
See blood everywhere
Feeling my heart beating faster than the sun
If it would shine.
I was running fast, feeling scared
Like the end of the world
Is going past me.
The war is happening and I'm still lonely
I just believe this should stop
I wish it's done
I wish it's finished
So how you see
I am a Benevolentia!
I love most of the people
I don't want them to die
I love by heart
Feeling the war
It will finish one day
Because I believe so.
Wiping tears of my eyes
Feeling the horror
The sky is dark
Dark as the pain
I can't make it all go away
I feel helpless.
I don't know what to do
The fear is getting me sad
I can't hide it anymore
Knowing I'll lose you one day
I wish this would stop somebody.

Cintia Filipa Santos (12)
Sydenham School, London

A Swallow

A swallow dips and dives,
Tracing pictures in the sky.

She twitters and she sings,
Racing with her gulp.

Happy and free,
They dance in the evening light.

The sun is slowly setting,
Painting the heavens with fire.

The journey has been long,
Filled with many a challenge,

But alas!
The resting grounds are in sight.

Down they all swoop,
And settle back on the rooftop.

Home,
The swallows.

Isabella Linton (12)
Sydenham School, London

What It's Like To Be Me

Me, I'm as excited as a puppy
But as cautious as a cat in the night.
I'm punctual like a clock
Though people think I fuss a lot.
I like to be tidy I keep things neat
But I still like to put up my feet.

My friends are like a gem
I would catch a star for them.
And my mum, oh my mum
She is just my mum
There is only one.

There's always rhythm in my feet
And in my head a tapping beat.
All day long I'm dancing
Twirling, whirling, prancing.
But if you come
I'll sit down quick
Because the thought of performing
Makes me feel sick.

Noko Armstrong Muhena (11)
Sydenham School, London

Little Miss Perfect

Little Miss Perfect
There is no one I hate more
Thinks she is terrible at everything, for sure
Little Miss Perfect
Thinks she is so funny
Rolling in all of her money
Little Miss Perfect
Has everyone sold
Living in her perfect little world
Little Miss Perfect
Thinks she is so bad
She gets all As and then acts all sad
Little Miss Perfect
Such a hypocrite
Constantly feeling like she doesn't fit
Little Miss Perfect
Always humble-bragging
Left all her so-called friends like me behind lagging
Little Miss Perfect
My hatred for her.

Mya Onwugbonu (14)
Sydenham School, London

Love, Anonymous

My daisy in the dust,
My ruby in the ruins,
Tugging on my heart strings,
Touch light as cupid in flight,
My night and my day,
The woes of the past have fled,
Leaving their tender places vacant,
And in its body grows a passion so deep I have to fight,
Wrestle with affection to keep my love a deathly secret,
Through sickness and anger, till death do me part,
Watching you, watching me,
Every dawn and every dusk,
100 nights awake, dreaming,
You mock me with your presence,
Not knowing but still believing in the recognition of but 3 words spoken,
A rose blooming, fuelled by a breath-taking temptation,
The cause of my heart to break,
It grows more passionate by the hour,
An enraging storm becoming harder to contain,
A thriving love in the murkiest but purest place in my heart,
My nightmare and my summer night delusions,
Midnight slumber and a gay daydream,
Not daring to name it by the word of love, acquaintance or friend,
There's nothing to stop me yet nothing to free me,
I keep my love anonymous, I keep my heart at bay,
All for you and all for me,
But you'll always be the light in my day.

Abby Reyes (11)
Sydenham School, London

I Wish I Could Be...

Depression,
Sadness,
Anger,
I feel those,
I wish people knew how I feel,
But no one understands how I feel,
I feel,
Depressed,
Sad,
Angry.

Why can't I have a smile?
Someone to put one on my face,
I want to feel,
Grander,
Happier,
Different.

I wish I felt that way,
Am I the only one who feels this way,
I want to be,
Grand,
Happy,
Different.

Ellen Gorman (12)
Sydenham School, London

Love And Peace

L ove
O pportunity
V ery
E motional

A ngry
N ervous
D eceptive

P eaceful
E ars
A nxious
C louds
E yes

Love is romantic
Love is something you do in pairs
Peace is nice
Peace is soft
Peace makes you feel relaxed
Love is emotional
Love makes you nervous, angry and sometimes anxious
Peace sometimes makes you feel like an anxious cloud.

Kasey Hilton-Ash (12)
Sydenham School, London

The Youthful Night

She felt immortal and indestructible
They drove down the neon green tunnel
The air was crisp and clear
The smell was sweet scent like cinnamon, roses, honeysuckle
She stood up in the loading bay
Hands high in the air
The breeze on her fingertips
The wind in her hair
The flapping of her clothes
She felt infinite
They came out of the tunnel full of life and buzzed with excitement.
They knew that life had meaning and that it should be fulfilled.

Eleanor Mildenhall (12)
Sydenham School, London

Dance Like No One's Watching

Blood, sweat and tears
Pounding music in my ears
I dance for laughter
I dance for love
I dance for hope
I am a dancer
I create dreams.

I twirl, dream, move and sway
Even though it's not perfect, I dance all day
I cannot judge
I cannot hate
I can only be joyful and that is why I dance.

I dance my best, don't compare me to the rest
I've learnt if you take more chances, you'll learn more dances.

Sienna Victorin (11)
Sydenham School, London

Strawberries

Strawberries, strawberries
You're my favourite fruit
Strawberries, strawberries
You're very cute
Strawberries, strawberries
You're extremely juicy
Strawberries, strawberries
I'll name you Lucy
In Spanish you're fresa
In French you're fraise
Strawberries, strawberries
I love you so much
Strawberries, strawberries
I'll see you at lunch.

Lanya Ghafour
Sydenham School, London

Dilligent Not Divergent

People surrounding me
Work my way through
The effort put in always
Compared to you.
I work along paths with my head held high
I'm diligent not divergent
And here's why.
My life has changed since
Entering this world
I've become a different girl.
I may be intelligent
But here's why.
I am diligent not divergent.
And that is no lie.

India Roche (12)
Sydenham School, London

Fear, Anger, Hope And More

It was dark.
I could not see anything.
It was so close but so far.
One minute it was in sight, the next it was not.
Snap!
What was that noise?
I'm meant to be alone.
Snap! Snap!
He's here.
He's found me.
My biggest fear.
The past is back to haunt me.
To destroy me.
I do not fear anything . . .
Anything . . .
Anything . . . but him.

No!
Leave me alone!
I don't want to talk to you.
You're nothing to me.
You're dead to me.
I'm tried of crying myself to sleep.
I'm tired of trying to impress you.
I'm tired of being unloved.
I'm tired of being abused.
I'm tired of hiding scars, physical and mental.
I'm tired of just . . . of just . . . everything!
Just leave me alone . . .
Please . . .
Just leave me alone . . .
I beg you . . .
Just. Leave. Me. Alone!

Here I sat.
On my balcony.
Watching the sunset . . . it was a beautiful moment
A beautiful sight . . .
It felt . . . I don't know . . . it felt . . . it felt . . . weird.
Because I have never noticed it before . . .

I never noticed it because I never had time to . . . I guess
I never had time to notice the simple things in life.
Because I was always on the run,
Hiding from him.
Hiding from the thing that one day would make me the happiest.
Yes . . .
The saying is true
Keep your friends close but your enemies closer.
My enemy was the one that showed me love,
That showed me happiness
And to stop running from your problems,
But to face them.
I faced them. . .
I stopped running from him
I . . . I listened to him
He told the truth
Or . . .
He told a lie
I don't care right now
Because I am in his arms watching the sunset.
I am in his warm embrace
Not no other man's,
And the truth right now is that I am happy.

Happy . . .
I can finally say that I am happy with a smile on my face.
I am happy that I am in love
That I found someone to love me
To give me everything that I want . . .
To show me things that I never imagined
To make me feel emotions that I knew were real
He brought me here
And . . .
He is the only person who can take me out of it.

It was that time of year again
The time of year where families get together for dinner.
Neighbours become friends
Friends become best friends.
Enemies become lovers . . .
Well in my case they do
Just the thought of him makes me happy.
No this time is not Christmas,

It is New Year.
The day of hope, joy and more.
The day people make plans that they promise to keep.
But fail
Breaking it after a few days/weeks/months
New Year resolutions are hard to keep
I know that for a fact
But this year I promise to keep my promise
Because it is not hard to keep
It's simple.
To be a more open person,
To be more open to doing different things.
Like . . .
Like . . . getting married
To the love of my life
To the enemy of my heart
The controller of my mind.

The master of my body and soul
No other man has the power of me like he does
And the truth is . . . he has always had it
And he knew he had it.
He just had to find a way to use it
He uses . . .
He uses it to make me do what he wants
To make me see what he sees
To make me want what he wants
To make me have the same beliefs as him
To hope the same things that he hopes for
He makes sure that we see eye to eye
That we connect both physically and mentally
And to tell the truth I am happy about it.
It gives me hope
Something to believe in.
It gives me faith
Faith that I never knew existed.
Faith, hope, love, anger and fear.
They are all needed in life
They control life

You can't love someone without fearing them
You can't have faith in someone without having hope in them
And . . .
You can't be angry at someone without loving them
And having fear for them . . .
That's what I learned
And . . .
That's what I will teach.

Sharifa Jackson-Douglas (12)
Sydenham School, London

The Day She Left Me

Looking back at this makes me cry
Almost close down even
The thought of it scares me
That it will happen to me too.

She couldn't do anything to stop it
We tried everything
And the day she left us came
She was the greatest mum in the world.

That's when I realised it was all real
It wasn't a dream, it wasn't a fake
The realness tripped me up
And I cried for days on end.

I couldn't help it
Streams of water poured out of my eyes
And when I went back to school
Everyone kept staring and trying to comfort me.

That only reminded me
What really happened . . .

Miriam Alston (12)
Sydenham School, London

Limerick

There was a young girlie from Cork
Who had an obsession with pork
She said to her friend
'This obsession must end,'
Then she fed all her food to a stork.

Carlotta Gooding
Sydenham School, London

Be Happy

Be happy, do you know why? Because what's the point of life if we're not?
Be happy, even though it's not all the time, life's a roller coaster ride.
Once you're up and then you're down.
Be happy, you are not famous, who needs all that attention?
Be happy, because you are amazing, just keep that in mind.
Be happy, you can't change yourself, so don't even try.
Be happy, life is great! Sure it has its ups and downs.
Be happy, just try to be you, don't follow the crowd.
Be happy, do what you want and make yourself proud.

Meghan Sarris
Sydenham School, London

The Ghost

The ghost knives forward as if his only guide is the sweet release of air,
A phantom lost to humanity's clutches, a remnant of uncare,
The bruised clouds far about seem to succumb to distaste,
For he, the ghost, is one to come far too late.

A spirit unseen under the invisible sheets: a lion's lair,
A wisp of a dream, foreshadowed a nightmare,
The blossom trees shake and he clutches branches,
Filtering through light's desperate tarnishes.

The girl puts down her pen and focuses a stare,
On her thoughts so uncollected, a jigsaw puzzle's dare,
She tries to see him, white cloaks, a grey mare,
A look out of her window, but he is not there.

A daydream of unplanned acidity, he had disappeared,
Angry and spiteful, yet a conceal so well engineered,
She waits for him to return, shrouding her surrender,
Ink pot at the ready, all to remember.

The journeying tales of friend and foe,
The hate of a hiding place,
The invisibility that marks surreality,
Supernaturals to the gallows,
He ventures our minds, a seed next to sow,
And we must wonder,
Where next will the ghost go?

Kate Landa-Warner (13)
Sydenham School, London

Love

Love can be close
Love can be far
Love can be silly
But can also be hard
Love can make you
Pour your heart out
Love can make you
Hold it all in
Love can make your
Trust stronger
Love can make trust not exist
Love can be me,
Me and myself
Or can be shared with family
Love can be caring about
One another
Love can be hope.

Joyce Kadibu (12)
Sydenham School, London

Watch Out

Watch out!
My world is falling apart.
Crumbling, tumbling in the dark.
Shadows lurk around in the mist,
As they lure you in with a goodnight's kiss.
The dark is out, it's not going back in.
It's here to feed on your fear deep within.
It's killed, taken and cursed my land.
It will come and take all it can.
So watch out for the dark, it's coming for you.
Yes, watch out for the dark, trust me it's true.

Nayah Kelly (12)
Sydenham School, London

We Are Temperantia

We are strong, we are proud,
We are Temperantia, sing it loud.

We risk our lives just for fun,
Come and join us everyone.

We always try our hardest when put to the test,
To prove who is the very best.

We are strong, we are proud,
We are Temperantia, sing it loud.

Georgia Pomfret Bannerman (12)
Sydenham School, London

From Within

It's painful,
It's deep,
It comes from within,
It fills you up with sin,
You keep it down,
Hidden inside,
Until one day you decide,
It's all too much,
It has to go,
So up it rises,
And out it goes,
But nobody knows,
Where it goes,
But don't be surprised,
When they look into your eyes,
You were the one that shouted,
You were the one that cried,
I bet you didn't know it,
Because it came from inside.

Amelie Mutton (12)
Sydenham School, London

Rowing A Poem

A sea as blank as paper
Surrounds my lonely boat
Despite that I had hoped for storms
I don't struggle to stay afloat.

I start to row with helpless splashes
My oars scrape the sky
But instead of forward I go backwards
'I'd rather drown!' I cry.

I try again, more fluid now
I close my eyes in pride
When I open them I'm spinning
As if caught in a tide.

'It's hopeless, I'll never row again!
The storms are gone I bet
No! One more try
Come on now, you can do it yet.'

I grasp the oars and plunge them in
And pull them back, my friend
With all my might I carry on
Hercules' strength I lend.

And soon I find the waves have come
They crash in crazy rage
I'm rowing, knowing
I'm no longer looking at a blank page.

Saoirse Spy (13)
Sydenham School, London

Misty Mirror

Misty Mirror, Misty Mirror,
May I look upon you?
When I search for the answer,
Tell it to me quick.

Misty Mirror, Misty Mirror,
Reflect my beauty back,
I may not be the prettiest,
But at least I try my hardest.

Misty Mirror, Misty Mirror,
I've placed you on the wall,
You are there for purpose,
No soul will make you fall.

Misty Mirror, Misty Mirror,
You are such a distraction,
You cause me so much trouble,
It changes my expression.

Misty Mirror, Misty Mirror,
May I look upon you?

Leonie Halle Rodney (14)
Sydenham School, London

Dissimilis

Dissimilis is with me
The faction which is free
So let's go out to find what we're about
To get our personality.

There's not so much of us
We have to work together
To fight us through the night or even the weather.

We need to recruit more people
To build us a bigger group
To become our own proper faction
So we can rule this thing.

Chante Dacres (12)
Sydenham School, London

Temperantia

Bravery is the number one key to be running around here freely.
My heart is pumping out of my chest, I can barely take another step.
Bullets are falling with one minute in-between,
That's how much time I have to not get any injuries.
My breaths are going deeper and deeper, soon I'll be just one skinny figure.
My sight is going thinner and thinner, I can't even see my pinky finger.
A hand stretched out to pull me in, some hope had finally started to begin.
We're moving slowly on this train then I slowly begin to rebuild my faith.
I can't believe I am free from all that pain and misery.
Becoming fearless isn't the point, it's about experiencing joy.
Being dauntless doesn't make you mad, it just makes you have a more crazy side than everyone else has.
So have an adventure and become dauntless today.
I promise you will have a smile on your face!

Kayla Williams
Sydenham School, London

Oh Sweet Strawberry

You are the sugary one
Red as a ruby
Succulent and mouth-watering
A coloured coat
You can taste it from the tip of your tongue
Oh strawberry, the tasty one
How I love you in summer
As you glimmer
You are the first fruit to ripen in the spring
Nothing is as comparable as you
And you will always be my juicy one.

Thagshiga Ragunathan
Sydenham School, London

Forest Labyrinth

As I walk through the silence,
The darkness,
Twigs crackle beneath my feet on the damp forest floor,
Birds are calling from high above in the entwined branches,
Mimicking each other.
Leaves are falling from the trees,
Flying through the misty skies.
I feel alone.
The only friend that I have is my echo,
Shattering through the haunting silence,
Calling for help.

Clara Keogh-Milne (12)
Sydenham School, London

I Am Dissimilis

I should be Temperantia
I am brave
I am angry
My head is a jungle
I am ready
I am willing to do what it takes
But I don't fit in
And I never will.

I should be Industria
I am smart
All that is in my brain is numbers, facts
I understand it all
I want to know
I want to try
But I can't fit in
I'm still too different.

I should be Castitas
I can tell when people are lying
I can see the sweat drip down from their head
See the worried movement of their hands
I tell the truth
I always have
But I was never one of them and I never will be
I don't fit in.

My head is on fire
I think in a million different ways
I'm not like the others
I'm smart
I'm brave
I'm truthful
I don't care what they think.

I obey no one's rules
I am my own person
I control me
I'm smart
I'm brave
I'm truthful
Which one?

None
I am cunning and sly
I slip through unnoticed
Everyone is looking for me
But no one has found me
I am feared by everyone
Yet I am a key
A key to freedom
I am Divergent.

Nancy Kelly
Sydenham School, London

Rose

Pale pink petals
Starting to wilt
No amount of rain able to quench the thirst of the bloom
Slowly
Slowly
Each moment imprinting fresh wrinkles
Upon the delicate flesh
Starting to fade
Fading slowly out of this world
Pink turning to brown
Stalk begins to droop
No longer able to carry the weight of the bud upon its shoulders
Shrivelled, dying, nearly dead
Going
Going
Gone.

Louisa Underhill (14)
Sydenham School, London

Human Race

The human race will live in space
A smile crept across my face
3, 2, 1 lift-off!
Excited, worried, so scared inside
If anything goes wrong
I have nowhere to hide
No bush, no tree or even a flea
To help me through the journey.

Ahead of me, the solar crown
Will I reach the Kuiper Belt?
Maybe not, here's how I felt.

I felt completely dead inside
In deep space there's nowhere to hide
Missing all the familiar things
I didn't know what space would bring
There is no Cubs or Scouts in space
Can you start them with an alien race?

Flips and tricks appeal to me
Now I live in zero gravity
They don't make up for a family
Unending darkness is all I see
I really wish it wasn't me.

So isolated and alone
It must be time to go back home.

Isabel Williams (12)
Sydenham School, London

Dear Framiriomi

You are as loving as anyone can be,
Your happiness will always shine through,
With your hair, bright as the sun,
I love the fun that we share,
It will always be nice that you care.

When you shed tears, we shed them together,
And will be together forever,
You wipe my tears away,
And I will wipe yours too,
For eternal happiness,
But that's not all.

Every time we speak, it rains down our lives,
It is nice to have you by my side,
Like a cushion to lay my head on,
As I know you'll always be there.

Nothing can compare to your beauty in the world,
Your soft sweet voice, the best of all,
You are twice as beautiful as you would ever imagine.

It is you,
It is you,
Who I love,
So true!
You are my best friend,
My life,
My second half!

Francesca Corp (11)
Sydenham School, London

Anger, Anger

Anger, anger, why are you here?
We do want you now
We always want you here
We want you now
We want you forever

Please don't go, please cause destruction
Please start wars around the world
Please start riots to destroy what's in the way
Anger, anger, we worship you
To be our new king to force us to destroy.

Tamsin Samantha-Jo French (11)
Sydenham School, London

My Poem

I love listening to music
I hate listening to my annoying sister.

I love the summery hot days
I hate the cold icy wintry days.

I love my PE lessons
I hate French lessons.

I love my family
I love my friends.

I hate nobody because I am a happy and kind person.

Shannon Linda Louise Holman (13)
Sydenham School, London

Lost...

Lost,
Drifting away in a black hole,
Stars surround me in the darkness,
Running for the door as it closes,
My eyes cry out to the rivers of the world.

Alina Kareem (12)
Sydenham School, London

Best Friend

You annoy me, you make me mad,
You tell me that my hair looks bad.
You mock me for my looks,
You make me read your favourite books.
You ask me out like every day,
TV seems like the only way.
You make me feel upset,
And hurt me every day I bet.
But that's you being truthful,
And just letting me know,
When it comes to the mornings and my outfit doesn't go.
You tell me I can't sing,
And that Glee's just not my thing.
But that's your way of helping,
And you just being you.
That doesn't make me angry, in fact happy that you care.
That feeling I get can only be described one way.
A best friend in the making,
A best friend till the end.

Jodie Lauren Powling (12)
Sydenham School, London

The Cycle

Same reason but you cry every season
Count your sorrows as the day goes by
Asking yourself why?
Why did it happen?
Was it my fault?
Do I deserve this?
You tell yourself just to forget
But the next season
You cry for the same reason
You tell me you have deciphered those years of hurt
You now know it was your own fault
Your own mind
That made those decisions
You tell me you are going to change
Am I right to believe you?

Same reason but you cry every season
Months have gone by and you are still stuck in that cycle
Of why?
Trying to persuade yourself that you can move on
But we all know the time has gone
For you to make up for what you have done
The people you love have already gone
Everyone around you has already moved on
They're living their lives with no pain in their stride
But then there's you
You're still broken from all those years
You were outspoken
Now you're trying to be clear

But every time you let that person back into your life
You remember your past
Remember everything you had
Had – past tense
You can't accept it so you cry in front of the mirror
In the early hours of the morning
Trying to let go
But I know you're far too gone to change
I don't understand how you can tell yourself
It's going to be alright
When the person who snuffed your light

All these past years is still in your life
Time has passed, so why can't you move on?
And start your life again.

Because soon you'll realise that you wasted time
Wasted time, crying all the time
Wasted the time of trying to make amends
You'll only realise once you're at the end
So please
Get out of this never-ending cycle
And realise
You can't cry about the same reason every season.

Rhiana Reid-Kanon
Sydenham School, London

Revenge

Margo, you tread stolen steps my dear.
You sunbathe in fame,
While I shiver in the shadows.
I am forever trapped, heartbroken.
You stole my sweetheart and replaced me.
You get all the credit,
While I receive none.
I do all the hard work.
I have the talent, you don't.
All you know what to do is shout and scream
And show off your good looks.
I will find you, Margo.
Remember, you're not safe anymore.
Your fame has put you out there,
Open, raw and alone without any protection.
I will set your fate, no one can ever stop me.
My little Margo, you can run, scream, shout all you like,
But you will always end your life with a fall, sit tight.
I will make no deals,
Just hope you're 100% lucky.

Laila Alao (11)
Sydenham School, London

Demon's Nest

Everybody wants someone to save them
From the demons in their minds
They want someone to slay the monsters
To numb the pain and hush the voices
But no one can save you
No one but yourself
If you think love can save you
Oh dear, I'm afraid you're wrong
Because that person who you feel for
Will try to enter your demon nest
To kill those creatures
But when it appears
The monster will have your face
And your love cannot murder it
The beast is a part of you
You must be strong and fight
Fight to save yourself
Calm the demons in the nest
Do not murder or fight them
They are you
You are them
They can't be slain
Only distracted
But you are strong so you can survive
And accept the demons
Enter the demon's nest in your mind
And accept your role
As ruler
Of the demon's nest.

Cadhla McCarthy (14)
Sydenham School, London

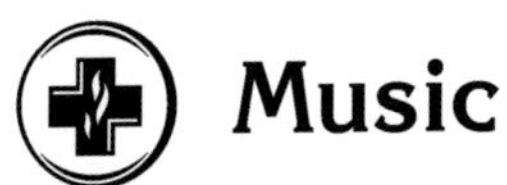

Music

Music can be loud and quick
Like a soft melody to my ears.
Hip-hop and rap, pop, rock 'n' roll
Music sings to my life
Music makes me stronger
Music makes you who you really are
Music gives joy and happiness
Music
Music can do no wrong
Listen
Listen to the beat
How it beats
Every second
Listen
Listen to the music in the stars
As it sparkles in the moonlight
Music makes us happy
Feel every moment.

Kylisha Moussa (12)
Sydenham School, London

The Rain

You try to protect what is yours from the rain
And every day, when the drizzle begins,
It ebbs at your heart,
As the recognition of what you left out in the rain spreads through you
Rising in your throat,
Filling your eyes with salt, water and pain
As you gaze at what you lost
Through the opaque glass of the window
The raindrops bouncing off the memories of what you lost
And everything you had.

And all you can do is press your hand against the glass
Watching the windowpane steam up
As you increase the pressure
Force out the memories, push away the pain.
Make your vision foggy and distorted.
But turning your back on tragedy
Brings no relief.
So you peer through the window
And watch your life crumple and disintegrate and dissolve
Like paper left out in the rain.

Every day you will remember what you left out in the rain
And those moments when you watched the droplets
Soak and drench what your heart arches for and misses.
And you won't forget those moments.

You will hug your knees close to your chest.
Touch everything with a new-found caution and shrewdness.
Hold everything you have left dearer to you.
Protect everything from the rain.

Orla Watson (12)
The Elmgreen School, London

The Real World, Our Home

The sublime thought of a pristine habitat is a hard thing to achieve.
A world without peace is like a baby without a bottle,
They both result in suffering and despair.

Poor, unfortunate souls who hide from their dreaded nightmares
Hiding their innocence in alleyways and under their coats
While the villains of the world stand on hills, beneath them swarms of corruption
Discrimination and greed
While the victims of these experiences crawl on the pavements
Feeding on any companions they can find.

Countries going to war over the last drop of oil
Like children bickering over what toy they want to play with
The world is full of dark, evil people.

Meanwhile, the innocence of a child shares the comfort
That they are safe from all harm.
When they sit down to eat their fish fingers
They are unaware that somewhere else in the world
A child is suffering.

This is the real world,
It is not perfect, sublime or calm
It's dangerous, fearsome and treacherous
This is the real world
This is our home.

Laila Ross Stevens (14)
Whitefield School, London

An Average Day In The UK

A boring day, I would say
Just another gloomy day
Clouds so dark
Across the floor dead flowers lay
A bright day
Could be the way
To spend my precious hours away
Just another gloomy day.

Kyrah Kanu-Cooper (14)
Whitefield School, London

Racism

Everyone is equal
Well, at least that's what I think
They judge you with your colour in just a little blink
'Ching, chang, chong, chink'
Oh please can I have a drink?
Cos this can be long, talking about those who really stink
Those stinking rats, judgemental
As if they're hoping for us to finally get extinct.

'What happened with your eye?
Did someone pull it back?'
Ridiculous night
But those rats come in a pack.

Respect is everything and that's just what I want
We are not aliens that can't understand
Nor prisoners, segregated from everyone
So stop saying hurtful words with your gun.

Laranie Ursula (13)
Whitefield School, London

World

The world is like an unequal scale
From rich to poor
When I opened the door
I saw the war
In the distance
People falling to their death.
I sigh and say
Why are we in this stage?

We look back at our history
But . . .
It's truly a misery
The world is like an unequal scale.

Hussam Al-Noori (13)
Whitefield School, London

Another Day

Another day you cry
Another day you lie
Another day I let you live
But next time be more wise
Another day you torture me
Another day you breathe
But next time be more sly
The end of the day I cannot deny
You are my little brother.

Mujhda Abed (14)
Whitefield School, London

Mother

M um you know me the best
O h God what would I do if I didn't come from your nest
T he days I cry, you're the
H ero in my eyes
E verything you do is for me
R emember I love you but now I set you free
For all the years you took care of me
Now I am not your responsibility.

Aziza Sheik Mumum (14)
Whitefield School, London

My Passion

Football is great, football is my hobby
Football is my thing, footballs and football players
From Champions League football to Brasilia.

Football players from Neymar to Ronaldo
Neymar is good at tricks and skills
Ronaldo is the king in football
Messi will always fall.

Slow down, no one can catch me
I walk too fast and the guys don't chase me.

Ronaldo watch your legs
Before you get an egg
Top right corner but I want it faster
Messi is rubbish, just too selfish
Never a legend.

Hamza Raza (13)
Whitefield School, London

Greed And Anger

Anger and greed, two things that kill and consume you.
Greed needs power, anger needs kills.

A great greed can become a great war,
War is an apparent need to humans,
We don't know what's good for us, we only make mistakes
And those mistakes can make us angry.

The greed that comes with envy consumes us
And controls us
The desire for more is a terrible thing
But we can't do much about it.

Luiz Fellini De Oliveira (13)
Whitefield School, London

The War

The bullets pelting outside my door,
As I opened the entrance, there was the war.
Men painted in patriotism, fierce with a roar!

They wore helmets, they were armed with guns,
They drove Jeeps and tanks which weighed tons!
By the farm there was a demolished church with homeless nuns.

When they marched, they chanted 'Heil!'
They slaughtered civilians then hanged them by a nail,
If you were caught speaking against them you were shot!
Then your body was dumped with others, left to rot.

Sudeys Mohamed (14)
Whitefield School, London

Couch Potato

Quiet and calm
Peaceful with the remote in my hand on the end of my arm
Sitting with a cold beverage on my plate
'He's a couch potato!' That's what others say
'Ooh that boy, he is so lazy
He sits on the couch still like a baby.'
Couch Potato, the name is known
Ring-ring, the pizza man's on the phone.

Jonathan Ndjoli (14)
Whitefield School, London

Hobbies

I love Xbox
I love football
But my mum doesn't like these things
I don't care but I refuse to follow her instructions.

I don't like studying
I don't like doing homework
But my mum loves to do these things.

I love KFC
I love McDonald's
But my dad doesn't like these things

Just listen to your parents please
Or you're just going to regret this whole thing.

Sharushan Shanmugalingam (14)
Whitefield School, London

First It Takes

The small vulnerable being,
Opens his eyes,
Waking up from a deep sleep, seeing his caring mother.

The small vulnerable being
Takes his first steps towards his loving future.

The small vulnerable being
His first words of an unspoken language.

The small vulnerable being,
The first soft food reached his new tongue.

Joseph Godwins (14)
Whitefield School, London

Shadow Of Life

No one knows the pain that had brought down this evil burden upon me
Years of suffering and continuous agony that life set as an obstacle.
Chains clanging, no sunlight and barely enough oxygen to sustain my life
A child of a beautiful home to a man of an orange suit
Life in the iron motel all because of my sinful iniquity
I remember it like it was yesterday
But the pain followed me all my life.
I would ask God for forgiveness but I know my wrongs
It will soon be time to meet my dad in the eternal flames below me
A life like this which everyone lives in comes with consequences.

Tyreece Gayle (13)
Whitefield School, London

Paranoid

Everyone used to tell me I was born an old soul
And I'm so violent
But there's this dream that comes across me
And I just can't let it go
There's still so much that I don't know
I keep my eyes wide open
There is this scar right next to me that is broken
I'm about to make my way
Heaven is on my left hand
I have to keep my eyes wide open.
Every day struggling, fighting with full strength trigger
Everything is upside down.
I'm just paranoid
My heart is beating so loud I can hear it
That's why I never feel like a daisy.

Jamila Ringim (13)
Whitefield School, London

My Console

My console is the best, it will always beat the rest.
The game is so great but it always comes late.
FIFA is a very addictive game
It makes all the other games lame
When my console breaks I buy a new one
When I set it up I feel as if I've won.
As my cousin breaks my console
I feel I've lost my soul.
I will never let other people touch my console.

Sabir Ali (14)
Whitefield School, London

The Man Who Never Gives Up

The man who never gives up
Will endure pain until the end
No matter how many grazes or cuts
He will always protect his friends
When I see him fight
He fills me with courage and bravery
If I get into trouble
I know he'll come and save me.

Faith Pinn-Bixby (13)
Whitefield School, London

Love; I'm Perfect

All the poems that I write
Seem to have the same insight
I'm crazy for this one guy
Who isn't perfect in any way
But I'd rather be with him every day
Than with a man who knows how to love
And expects more from me
Like some outstanding fee.

No, I prefer unflavoured
So I can add the spice
It's far more nice
I have an empty glass
And fill it with any drink
Don't you think
It's better with every sip
If you make it.

Francesca Barnes-Grundon (15)
Whitefield School, London

A Summer Haiku

Hot summer's evening
The yellow sand is shining
Mother Nature lives.

Razvan Dumitru(12)
Whitefield School, London

The Jeremy Kyle Show

Why did you cheat on me?
My friend killed herself because of you
Why are you so violent to my kids
Please stop staring.

You cheated on me with my friend
Stop hitting my children
You're a bad fiancée
I don't want you in my life anymore.

Ayman Choviovet Bensar (13)
Whitefield School, London

Summer Haiku

I drink lemonade
On a hot day with my friends
And I play football.

Vivien Bagi (12)
Whitefield School, London

A Summer Haiku

Magic in summer
Sunlight yellow in the sky
People chilling out.

Erfan Saghari (13)
Whitefield School, London

Summer Haiku

I go to the beach
And I swim in the cold sea
With my friends all day.

Vivien Szabo (13)
Whitefield School, London

The Things I Enjoy

My name is Jordan, I like to dance
I have always had a passion for dance
I also like to write
I love my Caribbean food

My middle name is Holly
When I was eight I liked to play with dollies
But now that I'm fourteen, I feel as if
I'm too old to play with dollies.

But in my eyes I see
That is a good thing
As I am growing up and
Am not a baby.

Jordan Boyles (14)
Whitefield School, London

To Mum

Tears falling down
All for you, Mama
You need to know
This is all for you.

You are our queen
And our joy.
Even the trees
Are all crying for you.

But Mama you need
To know you will
Stay in our heart and
Souls.

You were the one
Who taught us how to be
Normal individuals
And you were the one who told us,
'Respect people to get
Respect back.'

Mama you are the best
And the greatest of all.
No matter what happens to you,
We will be here for you.

And we all want to scream
So loud for you because
We are so proud of you.
You are the one who makes us think properly
And always wants the best for us.

Love you Mum!

Shnia Ako (14)
Whitefield School, London

Untitled

To me, the one who reaches for the sky
To me, the one who sets her hopes too high
To me, the one who's always left behind
To me, the one who wants to be set free
To me, the one who wants to please everybody, but me
To me, the one who has a different personality each day
To me, the one who chooses a different way
To me, the one who searches for the other half of me
To me, the one who's anything but complete . . .

Najmo Osman (14)
Whitefield School, London

From The Inside

Warmth surrounds me
In danger, I will not flee
Swirling, uplifting from inside
Rising, like a roller coaster ride
Keeping up, nothing can get me down
Nobody will give me a frown
Even if you try
I will not die
So, to all that are sad
Be happy, cause sad is bad.

Luke Brown (13)
Whitefield School, London

Endless

My eyes glass over
The windows to my soul.
My hair hangs limp
Wisps cover my face.
My cheeks are pale
Covered by glistening tears.
My body feels cold,
It's freezing from within.
My soul cries on,
'Til I'm hollow, hollow, hollow.

Ella Arends Page (14)
Whitefield School, London

My Black Is Beautiful

Oh Lord, why did you make me so black?
How come my eyes are brown and not the colour of the ocean?
My own people mistreat me; say my skin is too dark and my hair too frizzy
I am told that the best thing that can happen to me
Is to marry a white man and have a daughter that looks nothing like me.
On a holiday to Egypt where I think open arms await
A woman tells me to take my hijab off because I am too black to be a Muslim
I am either too Muslim or too black to be accepted.
Around the world my hijab is seen as my noose while my skin is a target
The colonial days may be over but your minds are still not free
Skin lightening creams to wash the Africa out of your face, sold on the soil of Africa
Hair relaxers to wash the Africa out of your hair, sold on the soil of Africa
Who told me to hate the colour of my skin, the texture of my hair and the size of my hips?
My black is beautiful, my black is beautiful and my black is beautiful.

Mona MacAllin (14)
Whitefield School, London

Stormy

And so I stare at the black hole of darkness I face every day.
It's comfortably intimidating and calmly threatening.
It scares me at night, it haunts me at pure daylight.
It follows my shadow and my fragile silhouette.
The weakened silhouette tears apart on the floor.
Knees slowly cracking and snapping.
Hands now become leaves – shaking violently in the wind.
My only friend is the weather,
We cry together in the loneliest of times,
And break down when it's just too much.

Bruna Todi (14)
Whitefield School, London

Exam Stress

Happiness and anger all at once
I cannot think straight
It's too overwhelming
It seems like I'm the only one.

Studying and stressing
Well that's the worst part
My train is not working
A breakdown is occurring

The clock is ticking
My time has run out
I've studied too hard for this
I cannot fail again.

Karina Saniuk (13)
Whitefield School, London

The Broken Earth

Why
Do we have to destroy
Our home, our world, our planet?
Nature, at its most beautiful and lively
Look around you! What do you see?
Trees once stood with their heads held high
Now cruelly beheaded, murdered and mashed to a wasted pulp
For no reason
Open your eyes, they're your friend not foe
Helping you breathe every second
Water: as pure as untrodden snow
You may think but that's not the case
Waterfalls lapping gently on the pebbles
Now a rare breathtaking sight.
Cars, lights, phones have become a necessity
CO2 reigns upon the world
I'm sure you'll all agree that your house is a gleaming whistle
So why is everyone ignorant to the state of the planet
Surely that's your home too?

Krinal Dhiru (14)
Whitefield School, London

Broken Love

I thought we were very close,
But no!
I'm even closer to my left toe.

You're such a disgrace,
Tie your shoelace,
No, actually trip and fall,
You'll have too many injuries to play football!
But you can't even play football!

You don't deserve someone like me,
I don't need you and you will see,
When you come begging again,
I'll just tell you to stand in the rain,
Because I don't need you!

All you want is nice hair and body,
I don't have all that, I am sorry,
But I am who I am,
Even if I am as fat as a lorry, why should I be sorry?
It's personality that counts most!

Little reminder;
If you dare break any other girl's heart in their faces,
When I hear about it, watch out
Because I'll mess up your teeth then you'll need braces!

Okay, not going to waste any more time,
Took me twenty minutes to make this rhyme!

Sharmin Akhtar (12)
Whitefield School, London

Why?

You inscribed pain into my heart
Destroying all those beautiful memories,
As if Heaven was the new Hell.
You left me with nothing all alone.
But I had loved you,
Nothing could change that,
I was sure of it.

Letting you in again, was my biggest mistake
I was so happy.
I thought you had changed for the good.
A single flower growing on an empty field
I gave you my all,
And you threw it right back at me.
I guess, I should have known better.

I mean:
Your touch made my blood run cold.
Your kisses left scars on my skin.
When you looked at me I turned into a block of ice.
And when I felt your presence it was like the sky was crumbling down.
You will be the death of me,
But, before I'm gone, my only question is why?

Malaya Rhiann Edwards-Roberts (14)
Whitefield School, London

I Am A Golden Toad

I sit on the leaves,
Adrift the dark murky ponds,
I am on my own,
I have no family bonds,
They are all gone.
The trees come down,
Because of a monkey-like clown,
My friends are falling straight to the ground,
Gone from my sight,
Gone from my life,
Soon I will joint the afterlife.
My friends are waiting by the door,
As my cold, petrified body,
Shines in the night,
Like a bright light,
As I am a golden toad,
Killed by the heat,
Caused by Mankind's greed.

Pasha Khosravi (12)
Whitefield School, London

Is Death Near?

Sitting in my rocking chair and I heard something downstairs
Slowly I got off my chair and got my walking stick
I went downstairs and heard mean mumbling
I got my cell phone and dialled 999.
I told them the situation but it was too late
They came running from all sides and tied me up
Once they looted my house, they brought weapons and
I knew it was the end
I knew I had no chance of surviving
One man with a balaclava came and stabbed me in the leg continuously
The other man got a baton and hit me repeatedly
Until my bone stuck out
But I realised it was all a dream.

Ayub Mohamed (12)
Whitefield School, London

Cheesecake

Every time I take a slice
My mind starts to drift away.

Go ahead and take a bite,
I am sure you'll be filled with delight.

Cheesecake come to me
Cheesecake stay with me.

Be mine forever,
Just like my mother!

Ishwaq Abdullah (14)
Whitefield School, London

You Broke Me

Since life and love came to an end
Never knew love would ever come to an end
The time you made me feel alive
Was just a bullet that came straight to my heart.
The time you promised me we'd be together forever
Was just another lie.
The time you'll realise what you've done
Will be when I am gone.

Milad Al-Kanani (14)
Whitefield School, London

What If?

What if you took the chance to know me
What if you act like you care
What if you wanted to love me
What if there was an emotion to share.

What if there was a connection
Past the wall of hate
Because through those words there is something there
To make us more than mates.

What if we had a future
A future for a lifetime
Endless love for each other
To think of you at night-time.

What if that question could be changed
Will our love die?
Because today is the start of something
Something for my life.

Nailah Mohamed (13)
Whitefield School, London

I Don't Know

I never know what to write about,
There are a lot of spellings to get around
What techniques should I use and how?
I never know how to rhyme like poets
I don't even know what's a sonnet.

I really want to stop right now,
Not put in the effort but give up right now
Just end this madness right now,

But wait . . .

I just used the rule of three
I remembered how to spell tree
Maybe I'm not that bad
Maybe I can write without going mad.

This is the day I will try
To unite the poem of my life.
Now I have the knowledge
To write a poem about anything

Although I have many things . . .
To learn.

Daniel Lewandowski (14)
Whitefield School, London

War

War is a hammer
It batters the life from all.
It cracks fragile hearts.

Peace is a hammer
It can knock you into shape,
It cracks hearts open.

A storm of sadness
It is dangerous and wild
And kills deep inside.

A storm of beauty
It is gentle and loving,
It calms the Earth down

War is a trigger,
It is waiting to be cocked,
Finally released.

Peace is an arrow
Fired from a glowing heart,
Now it will be free.

Jack (11)
Whitefield School, London

Equality

I wish that one day
People would judge someone on their character
Not their appearance.

I wish that one day
Women could be as equal as men,
They would rise with men, not be below.

I wish that one day,
Everyone would come together as white doves.

I wish that one day,
People would appreciate the presence of others.

I wish that one day,
The expression of anger wouldn't exist.

I wish that one day,
Life wasn't as complicated as it is today.

Taniyah Heaven Cameron (11)
Whitefield School, London

School Days

The sound of the wind whistled in the trees
Its cold breeze pinching my skin.
The river, reflecting the clear blue sky glistened
And sparkled as it flowed noiselessly on.
Tears poured down pale white cheeks
From all the suffering and all the beats.
I didn't want to go back to school.
With everyone looking at me like I am some kind of fool
The only option I had was to run.
But I knew it wouldn't be that much fun.

Faith Mbetolo (11)
Whitefield School, London

Angry

There is a side of me that you don't want to see
It takes over me
Devours my soul
My heart beats
I'm ready to down anything
Full of one smell of blood
So quick the whole thing happened
Until I knew
I was washing the blood off my heart.

Faiza Abdullhi (11)
Whitefield School, London

Love

Roses are red violets are blue
Some people think love is fake
But trust me, love is true.

When you're young
You won't understand
But once you're older love is more than grand.

Sometimes love will leave you heartbroken
There are also times
Where you can be outspoken – ouch!

But don't worry
Love isn't a type of mystery
But if you leave it for too long it will become history . . .

Jamarley Richards (11)
Whitefield School, London

Just Friends

Just friends, I tell them
But when they turn their backs
A grin hiding under my skin.
They don't know, 'we're just friends',
I tell them again.

Just friends, I tell them
But your smile gives me goose bumps.
It makes me shiver but you make me feel warm
They don't know, 'we're just friends',
I tell them again.

The smile that lurks under my skin
Have I told you?
It only exists when I'm with you.
But it's a secret,
I'm just friends with you.

It's just a poem
Maybe a story
Because we're more than just friends
You're my best friend.

Colline Crispulo (14)
Whitefield School, London

Sometimes

Sometimes I am angry,
Sometimes I am sad,
Sometimes I am happy
Sometimes I am crazy.

Every day I have mixed emotions,
Just like every girl in the world,
No one is different,
So everyone should be treated right.

Sometimes I am angry,
Sometimes I am sad,
Sometimes I am happy,
Sometimes I am crazy.

Millions of people are dying each year,
We should not be treated in a disgusting way,
Everyone cries every second,
So we should count and care for each teardrop.

Sometimes I am angry,
Sometimes I am sad,
Sometimes I am happy,
Sometimes I am crazy.

Everyone is important,
So we should care
No one is different,
So we should share.

Fatima Osman (12)
Whitefield School, London

Love

Without love in this world there will be a war
Love is like a connection heart to heart
It can never break, it's blessed with God's love.

Love is not like when you write your name in the sand,
It can be washed away but if your sweetheart's name is in your heart
It can never be washed away or removed.

When I see you my heart beats ten times more
You're in my heart until the end
I dream about you every day.

Aishwa Iqbal (11)
Whitefield School, London

Love

A million stars in the sky
One shines brighter I can't deny
A love so precious
A love so true
A love that comes from me to you.

She makes me laugh,
She makes me smile
All the time I spent with her is worthwhile.

We will never part
Because you will always be there
Living in my heart.

Danny Bagnall (11)
Whitefield School, London

Friends

As dark as night and as light as day
We will shine until we fly,
Hope to fly until we die.
Together we play, forever we stay.
Together we dream as a team,
Friends for eternity flying through the galaxy
Holding hands and plaiting hair
All the secrets that we share.
Do you know what you mean to me?
You're my world, you're my hope, you're my everything
Without you I will be too shy,
Without you I will wither and die
You're my friend. You're my friend
You're my love for life.
You're my friend.

Najma Ali (12)
Whitefield School, London

What I Like To Do

I like playing games with my brother
But I don't like playing games with my mother.
She is sometimes too busy to play with me
Because she is sometimes watching TV.

I like to play with my brother
It is so much fun
And all day we are under the sun.

I sometimes like to play with my little sister
But sometimes she gets a little blister.

Ismail Saghir (11)
Whitefield School, London

Love Or Loathe

Love is a strange thing,
Sometimes it is good,
And other times it is evil,
It can be an amazing experience,
Or it can be somewhere you never want to go again.

Whether you love it or loathe it,
It is always there,
Somewhere in the air,
Between people.

Hate is also an undiscovered feature
It is mostly bad,
With no sense of love or kindness
Often a journey that should only be travelled once
It can occur regularly or not again.

Isabelle Lewis (12)
Whitefield School, London

Loss Of Trust

My trust was deprived
My anger could eat me alive.

Friendship has aged collecting dust
A sin committed like lust.

Tearing away my own flesh
Blood drawn new and fresh.

People say everything heals with time
But I know it's a lie.

The seven stages of grief take place
I want it to be quick like a race.

I'm praying for the next day
But it's long like Fifty Shades of Grey.

I'm coming out shipped and beaten
And at last all is forgiven.

Bhavya Thapa (12)
Whitefield School, London

Football Gaming

F ootballs flying
O pponents crying
O wn goal humiliation
T ricksters' determination
B oss man goals
A bsolute trolls
L ying cheaters
L osers weepers

G iving up is not an option
A ccomplishing every mission
M ajor deaths
I nvisible thefts
N BA Masters
G TA hunters.

Antonio Shepherd (12)
Whitefield School, London

The Thought Of Love

The thought of love,
Has never been for me to think of,
But how else can I say,
At least I don't have to pay.

And the reflection of your face,
It makes me feel,
Like I'm in a maze!
Oh let's not chat about your eyes,
Not to mention when you look at me
I feel like ice!

They way you move,
The way you touch,
The way you look,
Can read me like a book,
However it looks like we're a never,
Oh it hurts to feel this pain,
Cos I've never felt it, never oh ever.

Our love wasn't at first sight,
But since that lesson,
I kept the memory like a treasure.

Ashanty Gouveia (12)
Whitefield School, London

Wintry Night

I see the flames in the fireplace
I hear the Christmas bells chime
I feel the warmth gently caress my skin
I taste the scalding soup travel down my throat, flavours explode in my mouth.
I smell the overpowering coffee fill up my home
I see the snow gently form a thick blanket on the ground
I hear the sweet carols caress my ears
I feel the stabbing cold seep through the windows
I taste the delicious chocolate chip cookies as they crumble onto my plate
I smell the mouth-watering turkey as the flames begin to die out.

Kushal Howell (12)
Whitefield School, London

Baby Love

Love is as emotional as a baby's cry
Love is as strong as gold
Love is as cute as a baby's smile
Love is as soft as a baby's bum cheeks
You're my world, you're my heart,
You're my everything, you're my love.

Ruweyda Osman (12)
Whitefield School, London

The Starry Night

The night is so dark,
That I can see a spark,
The light shining in my eyes,
Like the reflection of the moon in the sky.

The brightness of stars that shine so brightly
They look like a million Mars bars
The stars turning on and off as if they are light bulbs.

As I lie on the ground I feel the grass graze my skin
I look at the sky and say, 'Goodnight Sky, goodnight Sky
And till tomorrow I will see you.'

Aisha Farah (12)
Whitefield School, London

Sweet Potato

Oh Sweet Potato
How round and bumpy you are,
Oh Sweet Potato
I even have you in a bar.
Oh Sweet Potato,
You're never alone
Oh Sweet Potato,
You don't have any bones!

Ali Gashamee (12)
Whitefield School, London

Poems – Haiku

Poems are special
They can be long or quite short,
There are many kinds.

Tobias Garrett (13)
Whitefield School, London

My Dearest Friend

Oh my dearest friend
We've known each other for an ancient time
Remember, remember the good times that we've had
We've done a lot and more will come
Oh my dearest friend,
I miss you a lot, but the good times will come
Hope we can have the same fun
The time will finally come
And I can tell you what I want,
Remember, remember you are my dearest friend
Hope we can be together and have the same fun as we want.

Iza Chera (15)
Whitefield School, London

First Day

His brain sinks into a pool,
He breathes heavily,
His eyes pop out as he sees his new school
He gets bullied by a boy who looks like a bag
So then he starts to act cool
He gets beaten and left like a flag
Comes late to assembly in the hall,
People looking at him because he has a ripped bag.

Omer Zia (13)
Whitefield School, London

Tear

I wipe my tears
Every day and every night
And wish you'd never left me alone
But yet again you will never be back
Life without you is a shame
The days without you are a pain
Because I planned my life with you
But one thing you need to understand
Is....
'I miss you so much.'

Heba Aljoburi (14)
Whitefield School, London

Say...

Shots in the streets
Shots every day
Something I can't control
All I can do is complain.

They took you away from me
They don't know what I feel
I wish it was a dream
But unfortunately it is real.

Say you're here
Say you're not gone,
Say . . .

Adelino Neves (14)
Whitefield School, London

Football

F ootball is a round thing
O bject of some sort
O ctagon, no not that
T echnology makes the ball roll
B lack and white of some design
A ll to see the ball
L ights up in the air
L ike it just doesn't care.

Tyreece John-Jules (14)
Whitefield School, London

Borrowed Space

I walked along the stone-filled path
Where people are buried under the grass
My mind is in another place
Thinking about this borrowed space.

My heart is pumping loud and clear
Why am I even here?
I should only come once a year
Even though he was so dear.

I turn my head and say hello
To the name that's carved in stone
He died before I was born
And I will forever be torn.

Amber Barnes-Grundon (13)
Whitefield School, London

Expressing Anger

Unwanted, left all alone, no one cares
And I did not cry
And I did not beg
But blackness filled my heart
Do you even care about me?
What's a question like that?
What's a silence like that?

And why am I still around?
I need to realise that my past continues to affect me,
I can only move on when I choose to confront my past,
Only then I can move forward with my life
Unwanted, left all alone, no one cares.

Diana Kalunga (13)
Whitefield School, London

Chicken

Chicks are the best, they like corn
Chicks are bored
Chicks are small,
They grow up tall,
They can run
Looking after them is fun.
A chicken cares for its eggs,
When there's a storm
The chicken keeps its eggs warm.
But when it's cooked
It'll be so luscious
That it'll be stolen by the man who's crooked

Chickens are the best.

Hassau Khoder (13)
Whitefield School, London

My Mum

I love my mum
She fills my tum,
With delicious foods and snacks,
She says goodnight when it's time for a nap.

She buys me clothes and food,
And punishes me if I'm rude,
She gets me what I want,
Even if I'm mad
I will never be bad towards my mum.

Kai Mulqueen (13)
Whitefield School, London

Unwanted

Lost in darkness
I'm all alone
So unwanted
Everyone I know is fading away
I don't understand why . . .
I'm just so lonely
So unwanted
I feel like I don't exist
I laugh, they laugh at me
I smile, they turn it upside down
So unwanted
So I guess I'll just go . . .

Dominika Pedzik (13)
Whitefield School, London

Chicken

Starts off an egg
Hatches into a chick
Grows to become a chicken
I feel bad they have to die
But it's fine since they're fried
Put on some sauce and some veg
Eat with rice
Enjoy and devour the flesh
You can eat it fried or roasted
Oh how I love my chicken.

Khadijah Suleiman (12)
Whitefield School, London

Why?

Why love her and not me
Why hold her in your arms while I can see
Why keep her close when I'm alone
Why is what bothers me

You talk and talk . . . Why
You care and laugh . . . Why
You meet eyes and gaze . . . Why
My love is taken by the sky.

My heart is broken because of you
But it's the little hints you give me
That keep me loving you.

Suldaana Osman (13)
Whitefield School, London

Emotions

Emotions, why do we have them?
Emotions, they give us pain which is a shame.
Emotions, they give us joy,
Emotions, they're everywhere,
Emotions, let us dream good things,
Emotions, control everything,
Emotion is the key to life.

Marvellous Egege (13)
Whitefield School, London

Dear Best Friend

When I wake up
My heart is blown
Knowing you exist
Is all I need to know
You lit my light
And burnt my fire
Do you know how I feel
When you are here?
Laughter attacking us
And smiles everywhere
There can't be a frown
When you are near.

Fatima Hassan (13)
Whitefield School, London

What Is Love?

What is love?
Is it affection?
Is it emotion?
Love is a word
It is a feeling
I guess it's for the weak.

Tayla Williams (14)
Whitefield School, London

Infecticus

I'm mad, mad with fun,
And feel like infecting everyone,
I don't mean to sound out of the ordinary,
But I do want everyone having fun
Under the sun while we run.

Kaya Reece (14)
Whitefield School, London

Teachers

Teachers, teachers,
I hate them all
Saying do this and do that
Never leaving me alone
Teachers, teachers
Annoy me the most
Always picking on me and calling home.

Taiwanna Smith (14)
Whitefield School, London

Pigs

Pigs, pigs, pigs,
Oh I so love pigs
I love the way they walk
I love the way they eat
I love the way they talk
My love for them cannot be beat.

Arta Nuhija (14)
Whitefield School, London

The Sea

The sea can be dangerous
The sea can be beautiful
The sea can be surprising
The sea can be calm
The sea can be tall
The sea can be fun
The sea can be full of life
The sea.

Emma Rainbow (14)
Whitefield School, London

Haters

Haters, haters, haters,
Why hate? Let the dove
Come into your life
And keep the peace.

Keep the hate away
And keep the fire away,
Keep the peace
And keep the love.

Muzammil Rashid (14)
Whitefield School, London

The World Ending

I see it before my eyes, the world ending.
Endless fires burning in flames blue and black
The world ending.
Burning craters fall from the sky causing only pain and havoc.
People screaming, buildings crushed
The world ending.
Gore is like an angry boar charging at its prey
The world ending.

Dennis Farruku (11)
Whitefield School, London

Family

Support, love and happiness
Is what you want
Family is the one
Who will grant your wish
Heaven is the place you will find them
Family closes the chains of love!

Jumaila Kalliyath (13)
Whitefield School, London

So What!

We were close friends,
Do you remember that?
We came to dead ends,
And you only sat.

You didn't even try to fix it,
I knew that there was something happening
You sat there and pretended to listen
But you just could not resist it.

After we broke up,
You didn't even care.
You applied to your need
And I know why I was there.

Sara Nikolli (11)
Whitefield School, London

Love Life

Love isn't a game,
It's also not fame
But don't be afraid.

Love is a life,
But not a knife
It won't kill you
But it will fill you
With love and happiness!

Tina Mootabi (12)
Whitefield School, London

Why I Hate You

I hate the way you talk to me
I hate the way you lie to me,
I hate the way you do your hair, and
I hate the way you wear your clothes,
I hate the way you make me cry,
I hate the way you make me think about you every day
And the worst thing I hate is that
It was all a lie about you.

Inês Oliveira (12)
Whitefield School, London

Strength

Anger, the everlasting flare of rage
Just too hard to control.
Anger triggered as quick as a spark.
Triggered from different feelings
Sadness and jealousy
Sadness the feeling you hate and despise
Because you don't want to experience it
Jealousy made by the soul and destroyed by the mind.

The stronger you are the more you understand
Always stand strong.

Akram Chowdhury (12)
Whitefield School, London

Love Above

He makes me feel alive
He makes me feel bright
I wonder where he is in the big bright sky
Even though we haven't met our feeling is as strong
As a big red heart
He knows that I am his because he's got my heart.

Mate Becker (12)
Whitefield School, London

Sore War

War
So sore
Soldiers leave
And
Some never come back
People sacrifice
Their lives for
Knives of lives
Sore
Food portions are low
Children are hungry for food
and
Thirsty for water
Because of war
Why oh why is war so sore.

Rai Hussein Al Zarif El Bobo (12)
Whitefield School, London

Homer's Friend Issue

The Simpsons are a colourful bunch,
There's one, fat Homer, he loves his lunch,
Mischievous Bart, clever Lisa,
Baby Maggie and Marge, who makes pizza.

They all get into weird adventures,
Especially Homer, who has terrible ventures,
Rude, sloth-like and full of dead ends;
It's a wonder that Homer has any friends.

Shivali Shah (12)
Whitefield School, London

Habagyoo!

I was walking through the woods until I met this orange thing,
It was a habagyoo
It had big smiling teeth and it looked like Pikachu.
It came up to me and said,
'Hi, my name is Totame -
And being orange is my game.'

We talked and played all day
And we didn't even need to pay
After we played, I found it hard to say bye
So I looked after him, so he didn't die.

I was walking through the woods until I met this orange thing,
It was a habagyoo
It had big smiling teeth and it looked like Pikachu.
I let him play Xbox and he changed his ways of fame.

Kareem Mohamad Al-Hamoud (12)
Whitefield School, London

Football Is Part Of Me

Football is part of me
The ball goes round and round
My brain goes round and round
When I'm playing football I never frown.

Whether we win or lose
I've still got my love for football shoes
Even if I have got a big bruise.

If I'm playing in the rain
I feel like getting on a plane
For example I might fly to Spain.

Ned Jones (12)
Whitefield School, London

A Forbidden Love

Our love is like Romeo and Juliet's story
It is a forbidden love,
Every day I think about you in my sleep, dreams and at home
You are the wings beneath my arms.
Wherever you are I am here for you my love, my cherub,
My life is incomplete without you.
You are my destiny, my Prince Charming
When I see your face it reminds me of kittens and puppies.
You make peace, you want peace
You are sweet and our love heart continues to beat
Every step you take is not a mistake
You help me get my frowns upside down.
It is like a dove is helping us bring our love
Into a happily ever after
In the future I wish there would be more laughter.

Ciann Antoni (12)
Whitefield School, London

Falling

I am falling
Swimming through a sea of people
I can't breathe
How long is a second when it contains this thought
Just waiting for something to clasp
Head and shoulders made of lead
Dragging me down
My final thought
It's time for class.

Sahra Omar (11)
Whitefield School, London

My Drone

My drone
My only one
You fly so high
You reach the sun.
You are a spy
While you're flying
In the sky
With your HD camera
Your spinning blades
And your shades
With a slick design
You'll be mine.

Daniel Hasani (11)
Whitefield School, London

A True Best Friend

When we're together
It seems forever,
When I need him the most,
It's like he's in the post,
When something's eye-catching,
He's watching
When I'm crying
He's dying,
So comfortable,
As if we're in Heaven,
If only I still had him,
Then I would win.

Michael Okoineme (12)
Whitefield School, London

The Bright Side

Let's see the bright side . . .
The bright side of a rainy day
The bright side of a storm
The bright side of a bad day.

Let's see the good side of darkness
The good side of losing.

The good side of harshness
Let's see the amusing side
We need to fill the half-full glass
We need to find the good in us
Let's not forget the smell of grass
And it's not bad to be last.

Bogdan Balosu (11)
Whitefield School, London

A Summer Haiku

Summer sounds so fun
To me with my favourite
Friends. Days on the beach.

Siria Melillo (13)
Whitefield School, London

A Summer Haiku

Summer is so fun
I love summer with my friend
Summer is the best.

Natalia Pietrzyk (13)
Whitefield School, London

Summer Haiku

Summer is so hot
I love ice creams in summer
I love going out.

Wendy Monduka (13)
Whitefield School, London

Summer High – Haiku

Sun high in the sky
It feels as if I can fly
High above the clouds.

Umar Ringim (13)
Whitefield School, London

On The Beach – Haiku

When I listen to
A relaxing song and I'm
Eating on the beach.

Alex Vladut Irimescu (13)
Whitefield School, London

A Summer Haiku

Beautiful summer
Playing football in the park
The beautiful sun.

Alexandru Tortolea (13)
Whitefield School, London

A Summer Haiku

Hot amazing sun
Hot amazing summer sand
Amazing swimming.

Stefan Angher (13)
Whitefield School, London

About Me

I am as certain as I can be
I wonder what I'm yet to learn about me.

I do know I'm not the person I will be
Tomorrow nor the me from the past.

I am here at the moment
And that's all I can be.

That's all I can say about me.

Kayleigh Paice (12)
Whitefield School, London

Friendship

All of you are always there for me no matter what,
All of you are as brave as lions,
You guys are bigger than the Earth and can beat the Earth,
Our friendship will stay as strong as a bone.

Hosein Hassan (12)
Whitefield School, London

Friends

F unny
R espectful
I ncredible
E nvious
N ice
D iced
S pecial.

Prince Onyinah (12)
Whitefield School, London

The Football Acrostic Poem

F un to play
O ffside rules
O pponents
T ackles
B all
A mazing
L iverpool
L istening to the crowd cheer.

Amaru Redman (11)
Whitefield School, London

Summer Haiku

The summer is now
I drank lots of lemonade
It was fabulous.

Meriem Dahash (13)
Whitefield School, London

War

W herever you are going you'll always hear people cry
A nd bombs are always falling
R ight there, right there people die.

W hy do people want power?
A t least don't kill innocent men
R egret is all you'll feel when you hear the next generation crying for help.

W e all are cruel but have you thought about lonely
A nd alone families, that have broken apart,
R ight there, waiting for their fathers to come back and fill up their hearts.

Anastasiya Romanets (14)
Whitefield School, London

I Wonder

I wonder if we can find the pot of gold at the end of the rainbow,
Without making a sin.
I wonder about all the wonders in the clouds . . .
I'm soon waiting for it to rain.
I wonder if the moon and stars would
Still follow me . . .
Even if I took a short cut around the universe.
I wonder about all the expeditions of the next coming
As I would be buried within the darkest dreams
I wonder about all the love and hate galloping in the stables
However, the weakest horse gallops the furthest.
I wonder if we saw the staircase to our future . . .
We would follow the jungle . . .
Back to our past.

Debbie Paul (14)
Whitefield School, London

Just A Number

Just a number,
Old is powerful,
Young is weak,
Old rules all,
Controls all,
Knows all,
Everyone will be guilty,
Saying, 'I know it all'
But it's just a number.

Sumaya Chowdhury (14)
Whitefield School, London

My Teenage Future

As a teenager, I believe that I have a future
Which is currently blurred
But it shouldn't be like this
If you think there will be great bliss

I think people like me shouldn't think of the past
As it goes by fast
And we should be wise about the present
By 100 per cent.

As a teenager, I believe that people like me should think ahead
And not just stay in bed
As we're capable of planning our futures
Like being a pilot or a nurse

The future does remain unknown
And will stay like this for as long as we know
But people like me can change the future
If we do something different now for sure.

Emirio Syauqi Pratama (14)
Whitefield School, London

Lurking Revenge

I lurked within the shadows,
Dagger poised within my hand.
Within two simple steps across the room,
I lunged forward,
Stabbed him, and . . .
Dead!

Rishika Jain (13)
Whitefield School, London

Affection Or A Misdirection

Love, is it affection or just a misdirection
Leading you the wrong way?
You gotta hope and pray for the best to stay
And the worst to go away
Remember the days.

Where roses were red and violets were blue
And where love was intimate
Not just looking right through
No cheats, no lies
No goodbyes.

Not like today
Where partners are led astray
Just because of a social picture
Without the hashtag
#BAE.

Erizon Macani (13)
Whitefield School, London

The Rose

Love is the rose,
Roses hurt here and there,
And die without proper care.

Love is a petal,
Petals fall from roses over time,
And die when not on the rose.

I am the rose,
Take good care of me,
And don't let me die.

Albulena Mehmeti (14)
Whitefield School, London

A Temper Of A Man

Every day I go to school
There will always be a fool,
He will annoy or push me around
Until I fall to the ground.

I feel like I'm in a cage
But at the same time I go rage.
I can say there is no law
This could be the beginning of a war.

There is no game
I can't tell you his name.
If everyone is together
We could rule forever.

This doesn't seem right
But we're gonna fight.
When I am done
Nobody will ever run.

Mohammed Abdullah (13)
Whitefield School, London

Little Things Made Big

The shadow of a bright shimmering glow,
Up above, surrounding and protecting the lost ones.

The shouts of awe and amazement as they flicker,
Like a flash of surprise, they grow in size and shape.

As animal skin hung in a box full of hangings, are they arranged.

The black liquid flows out like unfaithful blood which is lost.
The swirls made can be praised or detested.

They fall with everlasting grace of a thousand feathers
Or crash like a thousand rocks thrown at the ground.
Drip-drop, splish-splash, all the way down
The teardrops fall.

Their dance tells a story of strength and ease
Its beauty lies there in its colour
A breathtaking gaze which fills you with wagging warmth.
It can restore life to the dehydrated and also take the life of the weak.

From a baby to a man, it grows
Fed, clothed and shown love.

The blooming can be seen as the 'beauty of nature',
Its owners sing a song of love
And work their magic on it as they cry out singing.

'Grow my seed, grow
Bloom into a thousand leaves
And provide for all'

Seasons come, seasons go
There is a time and a season for everything under the sun
But a time will come
When the circle of life has begun.

Wither, fall, the command is made
Years of hard work down the drain.

As the queen awaits her subjects
Poverty is around the corner
Waiting for its prey . . .

Deborah Adesanya (13)
Whitefield School, London

Feelings

I'm holding within
A rose in my cold, pale hand
In the middle of nowhere,
I'm now surrounded by monsters
Also known as people
They stare, they laugh
But why are they so empty.

My heart beats faster,
Faster as every tear comes out of my eyes
It just seems like I'm around a big bubble
That keeps popping out these feelings
Inside of me.

But they just laugh about it,
Thinking of a new feeling called 'happiness'
That make their life so bright.
But where's the bright colours in my life?
Have I turned off the lights inside my room.

I just stepped away,
Away from the crowd,
The deathless crowd that keeps fading
With their big clown smiles that bring me down
Upon them.
I fall, fall away into darkness
That seems loving, and hugging me around.

But yet, I fell out again
All lonely, weak,
But with a red beating clock
That can't stop loving, caring a lot
If happiness was a choice
Why am I still here . . . ?

And then, just then . . .
I finally saw the bright lights around
That were shining in my eyes
And people, the most loving ones
Standing next to me
They all questioned where I had been.

I would ask that to myself
But now as I saw the most beautiful light,
Like the star
I realised that life isn't perfect
As we wish, wish.

But we can make it bright,
Just with our positive thoughts
And maybe . . .
Those colours came from my head
That I was looking for.

Samanta Simailyte (14)
Whitefield School, London

Nan

My nan was with me from an early age
This is a bit like a book, as I turn the page,
She helped bring me up till I started school,
Where she wanted me to learn, and not be a fool
From babysitting in the early years,
To troubles later, when she would calm my fears,
My nan was always there with a little money to share
Then she became ill with cancer, and needed special care,
I did my best to help her out, as did my family clearly,
Because my nan was special, and I loved her dearly.

Sophie Hale (14)
Whitefield School, London

Empty At Night

Day turns to night
And my carefree grin turns into an unexplainable sadness,
Etched on my face like a tattoo.
And I lie in bed,
Thinking about all the things I wish I could say,
All the things I'm too afraid to admit,
Even with only pen and paper.

It's nights like these I realise:
I am many things,
I am happy and sad,
Outgoing and shy
Rambunctious and quiet.

But mostly
I am empty.
And somehow I know I'm not the only one
Somewhere in this world,
There is someone who will understand me.

And that someone,
Will not make me feel empty again.

Giorgia-Alessia Avadanei (14)
Whitefield School, London

Peace

Why killing and hating,
When you can love
And make peace,
Stop the wars,
And let's make the world a peaceful world
So everyone can
Enjoy the safe world.

Hussein Dahash (15)
Whitefield School, London

Blades

Blood dripping off her hand,
Her wrists are loose, her veins are cut
The tears running down her cheeks like endless rivers.

'Help me!' she whispered to herself
No one was there, no one could help
She took one last look at her wrist
'Why . . . Why I am doing this to myself?'

Her bloody hands soon reached her face
Wiping all that endless pain
She closed her eyes and hugged herself
'No one is here . . . No one to help'
The knife dug down her pale soft skin.

Oh once again, where do I begin?
Such an angel is now lost again
No hope of life, just endless pain.

Baby, baby please just don't do this to yourself
Pain is hard but you can win this fight
Put down that knife, put down that blade
I know it's hard but you're worth the wait.

Salomeea Olaru (13)
Whitefield School, London

Mirror/This Is Me

I am a traveller
Full of wonder, wonder
With a mountain of confusion
I ponder, ponder
Living this life
To get better, better
Like a growing crop
With a brighter future, pleasure.

Novilene Gatiw-An (14)
Whitefield School, London

Gone!

You're gone but never forgotten
Your soul is with me although your body is gone
We try to forget you but you're always here
Your body is lost but your soul is found
We miss you but forgive you
We thought you had your whole life ahead of you
My tears are dropping as fast as a speeding bullet
Your soul is trapped in a different world
But without you there is no hope
Goodbye Mr Teddy!

Kymani Hutchinson (13)
Whitefield School, London

Dissmilis

The birds are flying and the wind is singing
But what else is in the air
The huge body made from metal,
Jumping and jumping from cloud to cloud
There's the wings and the birds
But what else is there to be seen
It is big as fifty houses
So what is it?
What can it be?
It takes you all around the world,
Shows you new places
What is it that you don't know?
It's a plane of course.

Deluar Hossain (14)
Whitefield School, London

Money

You're always talking about money
Wishing you have more
You're funny
But you never realise it
Because you're always talking about money.
Money brings you sadness
But love brings you happiness
Word!

Suada Ali Ahmed (12)
Whitefield School, London

War

War is hell
No one is good in war.
In war no one wins
Go to hell
With the war.

You can't stop a war
No one can.
It's not like there's
A fan.

Old men start
War
Young men die in
War.

War is hell.

Bruno Strzemiecki (12)
Whitefield School, London

Atrocity

From terrorism
To discrimination.
Wars, wars, wars.
All troubles of the past.
Why bring them back?

There are things we can't stop.
There are things we can.
Tsunamis, earthquakes, hurricanes.
Yes, they kill thousands of people.
Unfortunately, we tend to kill people as well.
Tens from discrimination.
Thousands from terrorist groups,
Hundreds from hunger,
Millions from wars.

What happened to the cycle of life?
Birth, childhood, teenager,
Adulthood, old age.
Natural death
A normal life.

But then what is normal?
The usual state of a person's life.
So then killing 25 people a day for a year
Is normal.

The world's upside down.
I wake up every morning
Happy because everything's great
Go to school safely
Learn in school diligently.
Not worried a bomb would be blown any second.

But in Syria,
A second me
Wakes up with tears,
Brother's dead.
Stricken with fear.
No school,

It's burned down.
Mum's still bleeding!

I can just leave home,
At any and every time.
She can't leave,
They're still shooting.
I'm on my MacBook
Watching Netflix,
She's on the floor
Waiting for when she dies.

A third me
I had dinner yesterday like always.
That was her food for a year
I have a cold
It's resolved fairly quickly.
She has malaria
Her resolve keeps her going.

A fourth me
She's in America
She thought discrimination was over
Her cousin got shot last night
For breaking the traffic light
Her uncle got shot
Eight times!
For running away.
All black
What a coincidence?

It's not fair
It's not right
That just can't be their life.
My definition of sadness
Is their definition of 'I'm okay'
Why do I get a free pass
And they have to wait
In a never-ending line?
I want to grow up
Work
Have a family
They just want to make it to 18.

Partiality,
Brutality,
Monstrosity,
Atrocity.

Temitope Kalejaiye (14)
Whitefield School, London

My Cat Fiona

I have a cat
That is kind of fat.

She is grey
Born in May.

A female
Bought in a sale.

She likes to eat,
Lots of meat.

Three years old
Still not bald.

Likes to look at the sky
I think she wants to be a butterfly.

She hates to wash,
When she has to it's like 'Oh my gosh!'

I want to get rid of her,
But she has the loveliest purr.

Daniel Pawlak (12)
Whitefield School, London

Money

It can't make you happy
But can make you rich.
Do you know what's important
Happiness or this?

Are you blind
Or are you possessed?
Tell me what's all this?

But when your money is out
What are you going to talk about?

Hannah Wazir (13)
Whitefield School, London

Anime

Anime the cartoons of Japan
My favourite cartoons
With demons and angels
With amazing powers and lifeless people
Amazing fights going on
And memorable characters.

Denis Todoran (13)
Whitefield School, London

The Everyday Life

I am a very happy person
I like to laugh and joke around.
I sometimes feel alone and upset.
Singing makes me feel like fireworks are coming out of me
Because I express my feelings in the song.

Music and singing is
The only thing I can use to express myself.
It's my key to let
Everything out of me.

Mariana De Sousa (12)
Whitefield School, London

My Mother

You're always there
And I can't believe you can bear
My selfish ways
They have shortened your days.
I would like to beg your pardon,
So he can let me enter the garden.

You were always by my side
Whether the road ahead was narrow or wide.
You always helped me up
And you always filled my cup.

You were my light in the dark,
You were the one who guided me along
And the one who sang me a lovely song.
You were my mother and now you are gone.

Faris Seljmani (13)
Whitefield School, London

Dissimilis – Haiku

Killing left and right
Blood on the wall, red, crimson,
Me running away.

Malik Yusuf (12)
Whitefield School, London

Shadow In The Dark

Misty morning breeze
Shadows from the trees
Swiftly swaying leaves.

I see a shadow, I can see it far
Something out of the ordinary
In a small space that's sparse
I go closer . . .
Bending towards it, reaching to touch it,
It moves
Taking my hand back, I see something . . .
It's a child . . . a boy to be exact,
Sadness and melancholy fill his eyes
I reach out again, he moves back . . .
Why is he so scared?

Salamatu Hassan (13)
Whitefield School, London

As I am playing Minecraft
Somebody named Stribethe Killer kills me
And my friend Abdu 841

And now I am playing alone
With my friend
Abdu 841

Alone and alone again
Playing by myself.

Fernando Abreu (13)
Whitefield School, London

When your money runs out
What are you going to talk about

And . . .

It won't make you happy
But will make you rich.

Onjona Battiu (13)
Whitefield School, London

Magical, wooden
Strum or pinch to wake it up.
A fragile soul.

Ariana Zaharia (13)
Whitefield School, London

YOUNG WRITERS INFORMATION

We hope you have enjoyed reading this book – and that you will continue to in the coming years.

If you're a young writer who enjoys reading and creative writing, or the parent of an enthusiastic poet or story writer, do visit our website **www.youngwriters.co.uk**. Here you will find free competitions, workshops and games, as well as recommended reads, a poetry glossary and our blog.

If you would like to order further copies of this book, or any of our other titles, give us a call or visit **www.youngwriters.co.uk.**

Young Writers,
Remus House
Coltsfoot Drive,
Peterborough,
PE2 9BF

(01733) 890066 / 898110
info@youngwriters.co.uk